THE BIBLE SAYS

The Bible Says

JOHN HUXTABLE

Principal of New College, London

SCM PRESS LTD

BLOOMSBURY STREET LONDON

FIRST PUBLISHED 1962
© SCM PRESS LTD 1962
PRINTED IN GREAT BRITAIN BY
BILLING AND SONS LTD
GUILDFORD AND LONDON

CONTENTS

PREFACE

A FEW YEARS ago I gave three lectures to a confer-
ence of British theological students arranged by the
Student Christian Movement at Swanwick. I spoke
about the authority of the Bible. In the spring of 1961
I had the honour of delivering the Maynard-Chapman
Lectures in Westfield College, London. I chose the same
theme, recast the material of the earlier lectures almost
entirely, and delivered it more or less as it now appears.

The argument proceeds from the conviction that we
cannot fruitfully consider the authority of the Bible
without at the same time asking how within God's
ordering of things men are brought to see and know
what is true. I recognize that in such conclusions as I
reach I owe a very considerable debt to two great men
whom I know only through their books, Peter Taylor
Forsyth and John Oman. Although they came at the
problem from very different angles, I believe that in
their thinking about authority they were much more at
one than is often recognized.

In the following pages I am at times sharply critical
of the position taken up by Conservative Evangelicals
about biblical authority. I hope that I have in no way
misrepresented them. It is more than high time that
they and their fellow Christians who are at theological
variance with them sought to come to a better understanding of one another. This is most likely to come

about by honest and charitable testimony to our differing convictions; and to this I trust that I have made some small contribution.

In referring the reader to other relevant books, I have on the whole confined myself to those which are fairly recent, on the ground that they are probably more readily accessible to those most likely to read this book.

JOHN HUXTABLE

I

INTRODUCTION

1 The Problem of Biblical Authority

'THE BIBLE SAYS': in some measure at least that prefaces what for all Christians is an authoritative statement. Christian preachers of all shades of theological opinion begin their sermons by 'taking' a text from the Bible. Presumably this is intended to impart to their utterance an authority which the mere statement of their own opinions could never have. It is often said that the chief aim of preaching is to be expository, as if to imply that explaining what a passage of Scripture means and applying it to the condition of the hearers carried greater weight than a general discourse on Christian truth, loosely attached to some verse from the Bible, or without any text at all. In at least some liturgical traditions the reading of Scripture in public worship is prefaced by the words, 'Let us hear the Word of God', which makes more explicit what is the underlying assumption of much that is said about Bible Study and exposition, that through the Scriptures God speaks to his people. 'The Bible says' is often taken to mean, 'God says'.

Where this equation is made without any qualification whatever, the Bible can easily be regarded as a sort

of oracle to be consulted in such a mood as will accept
the consequent deliverance without question or reflection. *Scriptura locuta causa finita est.*[1]

For a number of reasons frequently discussed, such
an attitude to the Bible is impossible for many people,
who nevertheless regard it with reverence and approach
it with faith. They are to be distinguished from those
who assume that religion is no more than discovery,
that there is no reason to suppose that God has disclosed
his nature and purpose in such special events as the Incarnation and Work of Jesus Christ and the outpouring
of the Holy Spirit. The people we have in mind now
are willing enough to believe that in Jesus Christ God
has not only spoken his final word to men, but has so
acted in history as to restore the whole creation to its
destined glory. Nor are they reluctant to believe that
the Bible is in some special way connected with these
special events in which revelation and redemption are
so inextricably intertwined. For them, the Bible is of
great importance; yet they hesitate to call it authoritative in the sense just described. Clearly, they would
argue that the Bible reports what happened when Jesus
lived on earth, what prepared the way for his coming,
what followed from it; but they would assert that this is
not at all the same as the unqualified assertion that
through the Bible 'God speaks'. That the Bible is historical presents few, though real, difficulties; that it is
authoritative for faith and morals offers many.

Yet the notion that the Bible is more than historical
dies hard, even among those who find the greatest

[1] The problem is solved when Scripture has spoken.

difficulty in describing and assessing the 'plus' which must on such a reckoning be added to its historical character. It is difficult, for instance, to suppose that in some mysterious code form the books of Daniel and Revelation disclose the history of the world and the fate of men and nations. Yet it is equally difficult to suppose that, if the Bible has anything like the importance for the Christian faith which has been constantly claimed for it, it has no conclusive word to speak about the course of history and the consummation of God's purpose. While most Christians would now find it impossible to take what the Bible says about the place of women, either in their relation to men or within the fellowship of the Church, as the final word on the subject, it is, however, equally impossible for a Christian to suppose that these and many other ethical problems are to be solved out of relation to the Bible. The Scriptures are more than the record of what once happened and men once thought: have they some authoritative quality which makes them a final court of appeal, which invests their deliverances with divine sanction, so that to dispute their verdict is to fight against God?

It is worth while to note some of the reasons why this is such a difficult question to answer for those who cannot without a good deal of qualification equate 'the Bible says' with 'God says'; and among the chief of these reasons is the fact that the books of the Bible were written by men of like passions with ourselves. The way in which the Bible came into being has been studied with remarkable zeal and in the closest detail. Modern biblical scholarship has been illuminatingly concerned with the detection of the stages through which the Scriptures passed before reaching their final form. As a result, we are much more aware of the human factor in the making of the Bible than those of previous centuries could be; and it is inevitable that the question should be raised of the extent to which the human authors of Scripture may be thought to have refracted the divine truth they were being used to convey. The critical attitude known as 'demythologizing' may well be regarded as excessive and even dangerous; but Bultmann has raised in a way which cannot be ignored the whole question of the relation of divine truth to the form in which it is presented.[1] The human authors of Scripture were men of their day, using such habits of thought and expression as were natural to them: to what extent does this qualify 'the Bible says', as an invocation of authority? Can we distinguish, and, if so, how, between 'God says' and 'Paul' or 'James says'?

[1] Rudolf Bultmann, professor at Marburg University, well known as a New Testament scholar and an exponent of Form Criticism. He is chiefly famous as the advocate of *demythologizing*. His point here is that the biblical way of expressing truth is mythological. The word is not used to suggest that the mythological is untrue, but that truth is expressed in a literary form in which matters concerning another world are described in terms of this-worldly concepts, e.g. the Genesis account of Creation, and the NT teaching that the Messiah came down from heaven, was born of a virgin, descended into hell, walked on earth, and reascended into heaven. What does *going up* to heaven mean to modern man? The questions raised by demythologizing are: Can the essential matter of the biblical message be distilled from the form in which it appears? Must new myths be invented? Or are the biblical myths so inextricably bound up with the truth of God that we must continue with them? See e.g. his *Jesus Christ and Mythology*.

It is claimed by some that the human authors of Scripture were shielded from all error, that in communicating to men truth of such importance as is contained in the Bible it would be surprising if God has not taken care to ensure that any kind of blemish or mistake were prevented; and to this day, as we shall see later, there are those who regard the men who wrote the books of the Bible as having been the secretaries of the Holy Spirit. If what appear to be errors of any kind or manifest contradictions occur in the sacred text, it is claimed that these could not have appeared in the original autographs, and that, if these could be discovered, we should be confronted with a Bible which would be in the strictest sense infallible and free from all error. How such documents could be discovered or recognized once discovered it is difficult to see; and the whole argument seems a somewhat disingenuous attempt to take the literalist position into a realm where discussion is impossible.

Quite apart from that, however, any such attitude to the Scriptures rests on the assumption that the human factor in the composition of the Bible is negligible. The suggestion is that we need not be concerned with what we can discover of the personality of this prophet or that evangelist; we need not weigh the climate of thought in which his mind was formed and which it might be thought had conditioned his thinking. Nor does it matter, except for the better understanding of references to contemporary events and problems, whether we know the situation, the *sitz im leben*, out of which this or that book arose. It has been insured

against error. All that matters is what God is saying.
Now, what God is saying through the Bible obviously
is of supreme importance; all other considerations are
secondary. This, however, does not preclude the question *how* God speaks through the Bible, and *what* relation his word has to the words of men. Nor does it
excuse us from asking how God constrains readers of
the Bible to accept the truth of what it says. If we are
told that God has taken precautions to exclude all error
from what is written in the Bible and that its human
authors were passive instruments in the control of the
Holy Spirit, we have to ask whether the facts of the
Bible warrant such a far-reaching claim; and if we are
told that God has arranged that saving truth be written
down in such wise that the only proper response from
man be unquestioning acceptance—'I believe because it
is written'—then we have to ask what is perhaps the
most fundamental question of all, whether in fact what
is disclosed of God's ways with men in Christ makes it
at all likely that saving truth should be revealed and
accepted in this way. Ultimately, the problem of the
authority of the Bible turns on the way in which God
constrains men to respond to him in faith and to offer
him the obedient service of their lives. Before God's
authority all men must bow : but is that authority so
exercised that men are bludgeoned into submission or
left to sullen rebellion? Or is the victory of God's truth
so gained that the vanquished consent to a triumph in
which they have been constrained to rejoice? What
kind of authority does the God and Father of our Lord
Jesus Christ exercise? We cannot settle the problems of

biblical authority apart from this even more fundamental consideration.

2 *Interpreting the Bible*

'The Bible says' presents another difficulty: does it
mean that we may take any text as an authoritative deliverance, or must we not discover some principle of interpretation so that the biblical message may be made
clear, and the reader enabled to assess the meaning and
importance of the particular passage he is reading?

This is a serious point, not to be brushed aside
because it can be used by the frivolous to indicate what
amusing and even disastrous results can follow from
sticking a pin into the Bible and accepting the result as
'guidance'. What is really at stake is the question what
to do with such a book as Deuteronomy, which sets
forth some of the moral consequences of faith with
great power and yet at the same time seems to require
of men deeds which are sub-Christian. Is it right to
indicate the points at which the teaching of this book is
reinforced by the teaching of Jesus and those wherein it
is superseded by him who is greater than any prophet?
To pose the problem in the moral sphere is simply to
illustrate a difficulty with much wider bearings, for in
the religious and more strictly theological realms, in so
far as these distinctions are at all meaningful, similar
points emerge which drive the thoughtful reader to the
conclusion that whatever authority the Bible possesses
is not to be felt in every verse. Can we believe that it
was God's will that the Amalekites should be slain with-

out mercy? If so, was it his will in a particular instance? Or is it of general application even to this day?
If so, how can we reconcile this with the forgiving love
exhibited supremely in the passion of Jesus Christ,
which is held up to the Christian as the pattern of his
own dealing with evil men? 'Go smite Amalek' and
'love your enemies': which is authoritative? And how
do you decide?

To seek some principle of interpretation is indeed a
hazardous undertaking, since it may no more than reflect what we wish the Bible to mean to the convenient
exclusion of whatever is offensive to the modern mind;
and it must be admitted that not a little reinterpreta-
tion of the Bible is open to this accusation. At the same
time, it cannot be denied that Luther used his statement
of the doctrine of justification by faith as a yardstick by
which to interpret the Bible; and it is notorious how
ruthless he was with the Epistle of James. What Luther
did was to use the Gospel, as he understood it, as the
criterion of Holy Scripture. It may well be thought that
this is the constant task and opportunity of those who
study the Bible.

At the present time there seems to be a considerable
concensus of scholarly opinion that we may understand
the Scriptures as the record of God's saving activity and
of the moral demands which are involved in trusting
response to what God has done for our salvation. This
can be illustrated as well from the Old Testament as
from the New. The moral demands of Yahweh, as
exemplified in the Ten Commandments, are prefaced by
a reminder of what he has done for the emancipation of

his people from the tyranny of the Pharoahs (Exodus 19, 20); and a similar line of thought in the New Testament is found at the beginning of Romans 12, where St Paul turns from the exposition of the Gospel, which has occupied the major part of the Epistle and reaches its climax in the doxology at the end of the eleventh chapter, to a statement of the moral consequences of accepting the gift of life in Jesus Christ with 'I beseech you *therefore* by the mercies of God'. God, so the argument seems to run, meets men with gift and demand, grace and obligation; and the proper response to God's approach is faith and obedience, which are in fact two aspects of but one attitude of mind. The grace of God has appeared bringing salvation to all men, and if we desire to accept that salvation we must believe on the Lord Jesus Christ; but this involves being imitators of his life and being made conformable to his death. 'Faith without works is dead.'

It is possible, therefore, to argue that the Bible is the record of God's dealings with his people and with all mankind in grace and demand. It would be one way of handling the Bible as a unity to seek to understand any particular part of it in the light of that general overall pattern—to inquire of this or that incident, promise or declaration: what does it proclaim of God's grace? or what does it indicate of the moral consequences of accepting it, whether for our life in the Church, in society, in the home, or in personal life? This is not to suggest in any way that we excuse ourselves the discipline of discovering with the utmost accuracy possible what any particular utterance was intended to mean at

the time it was spoken. To handle the Bible religiously
and theologically is no deliverance from grammar and
history. Yet grammar and history are but the essential
beginning of our study of the Bible. Having discovered,
for example, what Amos actually said and what in his
circumstances he may be supposed to have meant, we
have to go on to ask what place this has within the
whole context of the Bible's witness to the activity of
God in the history of Israel, the life and ministry of
Jesus Christ, and the consequent work of the Holy
Spirit in the Church. The part must be understood in
the light of the whole. The words are not to be interpreted as our fancy dictates nor yet as invested with
some mysterious oracular sanctity, but as they bring
home to our hearts and minds some aspect of God's
grace and demand, and through them God himself
makes his appeal to us.

3   *The Inspiration of the Bible*

But is not the Bible inspired? Ought it not to be
received as belonging to a different category from that
of any other literature altogether? Strictly speaking, the
problem of the authority of the Bible is distinct from
that of its inspiration, and it is important that the distinction should be kept in clear view; yet it is manifest
that the two are so closely connected that they cannot
be treated in absolute separation.

(a) *Conservative Evangelicals.* The way in which the
inspiration of the Bible is understood in Conservative
Evangelical circles has, it may be supposed, never been

stated with greater clarity and vigour than by B. B. Warfield, who understands what he calls the doctrine of inspiration as the Church's claim 'that by a special, supernatural, extraordinary influence of the Holy Ghost, the sacred writers have been guided in their writing in such a way, as while their humanity was not superseded, it was yet dominated that their words became at the same time the words of God, and thus, in every case and all alike, infallible'.[1]

The word 'extraordinary' here is used to indicate that this inspiration is of a different sort than that of the poet or some other man of genius; and it is further claimed that it is different from the Holy Spirit's normal activity in the conversion and guidance of believers: 'Paul had some more prevalent safeguard against false-teaching than Luther.' And the difference consists in the inspiration of the *sacred writers* being 'such an influence as makes the words written under its guidance, the words of God, by which is meant to be affirmed an absolute infallibility (as alone fitted to divine words) admitting no degrees whatever, extending to the very word, and to all the words. So that every part of Holy Writ is thus held alike infallibly true in all its statements, of whatever kind'.[2]

Warfield was unwilling to attempt to define the mode of this inspiration, about which he claimed that the Reformed Churches have ever held that it is an inscrutable mystery: 'they content themselves with defining

---

[1] B. B. Warfield, *The Inspiration and Authority of the Bible*, p. 422.
[2] *Ibid.*, p. 420.

carefully and holding fast the effects of the divine influence, leaving the mode of divine action by which it
is brought about draped in mystery'. It is interesting
that Warfield was anxious to defend such a view of
inspiration from the charge of being mechanical.
Alongside the claim that every word of the Scriptures,
without exception, is the word of God, he would hold
that every word is also the word of man, so that while
we should be strong and uncompromising in 'resisting
the attribution to the Scriptures of any failure in absolute truth and infallibility', we should also be 'before all
in seeking, and finding, and gazing on in loving rapture,
the marks of fervid impetuosity of a Paul, the tender
saintliness of John, the practical genius of a James, in
the writings which through them the Holy Ghost has
given for our guidance'. It is in this sense that Warfield
believed that, while the humanity of the sacred writers
was 'not superseded, it was yet so dominated that their
words became at the same time the words of God, and
thus, in every case and all alike, infallible'.

Some further light is thrown on Warfield's teaching
about inspiration in this comment on 2 Peter 1.20, 21.
The assertion that 'men moved by the Holy Spirit spoke
from God' is interpreted on the understanding that
'moved' should be taken to imply that those thus
'moved' contribute nothing to the movement but are
simply moved. The word 'passivity' hardly suits Warfield's purpose here, for he does not wish to deny that
the intelligence of the prophets was active in the reception of the message. What he does wish to deny, however, is that their intelligence was active in the produc-

tion of the message : rather, it was active receptively, not creatively. 'Their messages are given them, given them entire, and given them precisely as they are given out by them. God speaks through them : they are not merely his messengers, but "his mouth". But at the same time their intelligence is active in the reception, retention, and announcement of their messages, contributing nothing to them, but presenting fit instruments for the communication of them.'[1]

It is Warfield's teaching which underlies what is written in the article on 'Inspiration' by Dr J. I. Packer in *The New Bible Commentary*, published in Britain by the Inter-Varsity Fellowship of Evangelical Unions.[2] This writer asserts that, while there is no ground for saying that 'an inspired document could not in God's providence have been compiled from sources by an ordinary process of historical composition, or passed through various editions and recensions before reaching its final form', yet it is essential to claim 'that the finished product is *theopneustos* (God-breathed), precisely what God intended for the communication of saving truth'. Moreover, this must inevitably involve verbal inspiration, 'since truth is communicated through words, and verbal inaccuracy misrepresents meaning'.

Dr Packer admits that these contentions cannot be proved : they are corollaries of the 'confession, which Christ's teaching demands and the Spirit's testimony evokes, that canonical Scripture was breathed out by the God who cannot lie. He who denies them thereby

[1] *Ibid.*, p. 91.   [2] In USA, Eerdmans.

shows that he rejects the witness of Christ, the apostles
and the historic Christian Church concerning the nature
of "God's Word written", and either does not possess or
has not understood the *testimonium Spiritus Sancti
internum*."[1]

It will be the business of some subsequent pages to
question and even deny such a view of inspiration, since
it appears to rest on quite unwarrantable assumptions,
It virtually equates inspiration with preventing inaccuracy : should the slightest inaccuracy of detail be
discovered, should any inconsistency appear between
two accounts of the same historical episode, should it
appear that the biblical account of creation be crudely
antiquated, presumably the Bible can no longer be
regarded as an inspired book. It is to this end, no doubt,
that some conservative exegetes compass sea and land
in order to 'prove' that there are no inaccuracies in the
Scriptures, that what appear to be historical incon-
sistencies are not in fact what they seem to be, and that
either 'the science of the Bible' is in keeping with what
is now known about the nature of the physical universe
or else that modern science is wrong.

(b) *The Liberal Protestants*. Those who have found
this too stifling an atmosphere in which to breathe have
sought some other way in which to understand how the
Bible is inspired. Not unnaturally, the question has been
raised whether it is after all possible to maintain that
the inspiration of the sacred writers was indeed different in *kind* from that of the poet, the musician, and
the painter. Are we not dealing with a difference of

[1] *Op. cit.*, p. 29.

degree simply? This at once focuses the question of inspiration on the experience of those who wrote the words of Scripture rather than on the words themselves. While the exponents of this view often venture the apparently unprovable claim that the biblical literature will bear comparison with the literature of any other religion and emerge triumphant from the test, they rather more often speak of it as the record of a deepening religious experience, and a growing awareness and understanding of God. Indeed, on this view it is possible to regard the Bible as the record of normative religious experience. The profit to be gained from reading it is a share in that experience of God: the men who wrote the Bible were inspired, and their experience of inspiration is in some sense communicable to those who approach the sacred writings with sufficient sympathy.

Such a view bears certain marks of truth. It is more in keeping with what we must believe to be the Bible's witness to the way in which God deals with men, than the view which Warfield set forth with such massive argument. However much we may be convinced that the primary emphasis in our thought about religion should be upon the objective fact of God's activity in revelation, a reminder that this activity must be perceived and understood by those on whose behalf God has acted is a wholesome corrective to an undue emphasis on the objectivity of revelation in which there seems to be little room for perception at all. And it is certainly true that, in so far as readers of the Bible are given to see the true meaning of what it sets forth, they do at least to some extent share the experience of those who first saw the significance of God's activity and recorded what was shown them.

While it may be agreed that this view of inspiration provides some advantages as over against that held by most Conservative Evangelicals, it must nevertheless be contended that its own defects are very great. What, on this reckoning, becomes of the uniqueness of the Bible? To call the Bible 'supreme among the sacred literatures of the great religions' seems to be to say something incapable of proof, since to compare the Bible with the Bagavadgita would be about as conclusive as comparing Salisbury Cathedral with Taj Mahal or a Bach chorale with an Indian lyric. And how is one to avoid the thought that something greater might appear in some future age, with the result that the Bible would be ousted from its priority or even superseded altogether? If it be argued that the Bible presents us with the record of religious experience of such quality that we should regard it as normative, we are still at liberty to ask whether this means that it is the best so far known and therefore in that sense provisional. If it be urged that the Bible has the power to evoke in its readers at any rate *something* of the richness of that original experience, we are left with the problem of those who declare that it does not have this effect upon them. Some assert that other devotional books are as 'helpful' and even more so. Some raise the much more important question whether this experience, however evoked, is indeed a commerce with reality. To say that 'the Bible is inspired because it inspires' records rather lamely an element in the devotional life of the Christian to which many could bear witness. But it can never serve as a satisfactory doctrine of inspiration. It does not satisfactorily describe or safeguard the uniqueness of the Bible. It is not sufficiently concerned with the truth of what the Bible proclaims and conveys.

(c) *A better way.* If we seek to discover some understanding of biblical inspiration more satisfactory than either of these, we may begin by recalling a remark of Dr Alan Richardson's to the effect that the question our generation asks is not whether the Bible presents us with noble ideas of God or leads to a deeper religious experience than any other book, but whether there can be found any place where God speaks to us. 'We want to know, not what men have to say about God, even if they are "religious geniuses", but what God has to say to men.' Dr Richardson goes on to argue that the uniqueness of the Bible is precisely in this, that it claims to be the message of God to the world.[1] It is in this respect that the Bible differs from all other religious literature in the world; and this claim is not affected at all by the open recognition that in the literatures of other religions there is religious insight of the loftiest kind. 'But the Bible is the only book in all the religious literature of the world which claims to find its significance in recording what God himself has done and said.'[2] In recording what God has done in his mighty acts for the salvation of mankind, the Bible bears witness to God's self-disclosure in this redeeming activity. This is his Word spoken to all the generations of men.

[1] Alan Richardson, *Preface to Bible Study*, p. 35.
[2] *Ibid.*, p. 36.

If we understand the purpose of the Bible in this way, we may understand the inspiration of Scripture as a complex in which four elements mingle. (1) There is the inspiration of those who were given to understand and record the divine activity in history. (2) There must follow the recognition that this inspiration is not only occasional in the sense of being given to a particular man or group of men at particular stages of the divine activity, but is also spread over the whole period of that activity through many centuries. (3) It must be frankly recognized that the human authors of Scripture were inspired to perceive the significance of what God was accomplishing in history and bear testimony to it, without, as the evidence shows, being given 'verbal inspiration'. (4) This inspiration of Scripture concerns not only those who wrote what we read in the Bible, but also those who read it in so far as they also are given to understand this divine activity and so be themselves addressed by the God who therein makes himself known. 'In the proper Christian sense of the term, the meaning of the inspiration of Scripture for me is that I recognize that God's message has been sent into the world with my name and address on it. The authority of the Bible means for me that God's message claims me, my obedience and faith; I must listen to what God says and hasten to direct my life in accordance with his will.'[1]

If the inspiration of the Bible is understood in this way, the uniqueness of the Scriptures is fully preserved, and due emphasis is laid on the givenness of revelation

[1] *Ibid.*, pp. 36, 37.

and God's activity through his Spirit in using the Bible to disclose himself to men and women in all manner of differing circumstances. The Bible is understood as a means of God's self-communication with men; and through it they hear his Word.[1]

[1] The reader may care to look at this matter further in John Burnaby's *Is the Bible Inspired?*

II

ROMAN CATHOLIC AND PROTESTANT ATTITUDES

WE CAN NOW examine in some detail answers given in Christian traditions to the questions already outlined. In this chapter we shall consider (1) the Roman Catholic attitude, virtually equating the authority of the Scriptures with that of the Church itself; (2) the teaching of John Calvin, whose influence on classical Protestantism is incalculable, arguing that believers recognize the Word of God in Scripture through the operation of the Holy Spirit; and (3) the thought of Protestants influenced by modern critical studies of the Bible.

1 Roman Catholicism and the Bible

No account of the Roman Catholic Church's attitude to the Bible would be at all complete which did not fully and generously recognize facts for which there is abundant evidence, however much it may be difficult for a non-Roman to see how they are to be reconciled with certain well-known official pronouncements. There has been, for instance, in recent years a good deal of translation of the Bible into the vernacular in several parts of the world. The late Mgr Ronald Knox's beautiful rendering into English is, of course, the best known in

Britain. We may take all this as evidence of a renewed interest in Bible-reading on the part of the laity in the Roman Church and of officially recognized steps to meet and even stimulate this interest. The liturgical movement has awakened interest in the scriptural basis of worship, particularly of the Mass, and in preaching. However, the Roman Church still forbids the faithful to read any version of the Scriptures published by any other Christian communion, and is obviously fearful lest the lay-man should draw too many conclusions for himself as to the meaning of the Bible. One Roman Catholic author makes characteristic expression of this fear in these remarkable words:

> Through Luther, although Calvin seems to have been the first to announce Monobiblicism clearly, the Bible became the arm of the Protestant revolt. A dumb and difficult book was substituted for the living voice of the Church, in order that each one should be able to make for himself the religion which suited his feelings. And the Bible open before every literate man and woman to interpret for themselves was the attractive bait used to win adherents. Not the solid rock of truth but the shifting sand of private judgment is the foundation on which Protestantism was built.[1]

The Protestant has never been as fearful of the results of private judgment as the Roman Catholic, although the extravagances of the 'lunatic fringe' have led many a Protestant theologian to admit that Romanist fears in this matter are not altogether groundless! What is cer-

[1] W. Leonard and B. Orchard in *Catholic Commentary on Holy Scripture*, p. 11.

tainly very noticeable in Roman Catholic pronouncements on popular Bible-reading is the extreme care
taken to ensure that the faithful are protected from
error. 'The Church is uncompromising in her guardian-
ship of the truth and she wisely withholds from her
children an excessive religious liberty which would
lead them into unwholesome pastures.'[1]

The other fact which must not be overlooked is that
Roman Catholic scholars take an increasingly valued
part in the work of biblical scholarship alongside
scholars from the Protestant and Jewish traditions. They
have made important contributions, for instance, to the
work of the Society of Old Testament Studies. Although,
once again, it is more than a little difficult to reconcile
the fact with the official theory, it is plain that Roman
Catholic scholars not only are familiar with, but to a
limited extent approve, the critical study of the Bible.
In the *Catholic Commentary on Holy Scripture* there
are articles on the Higher Criticism of the Bible and the
Gospels and Non-Catholic Higher Criticism. A good
deal of hostility is shown towards the evolutionary
theories with which the earlier higher criticism was
allied. Wellhausen and Harnack, for instance, are
vigorously attacked, not so much because of their
attempt to settle New Testament problems as because
they make certain dogmatic assumptions about the im-
possibility of miracle; this is a criticism which a good
many Protestants would equally desire to make. In
another article on the Introduction to the Pentateuch,
a documentary origin of the Pentateuch is not ruled out;

[1] *Ibid.*, pp. 11-12.

and a very liberal interpretation is set upon the Mosaic authorship. Karl Adam explains that Pius X's Bull *Pascendi* did not forbid the use of the historico-critical method, but rather declared that men should not make supernatural faith depend upon the results of this method.[1] Nevertheless, the enquiry of the Romanist scholar does not seem to be entirely free. He has to work in a realm in which certain results are fixed, as is evidenced by Père Lagrange's remark about the authorship of the Fourth Gospel, to the effect that it is not a question whether it was written by the beloved disciple, or John the Son of Zebedee. 'Ce point est fixé par la tradition ecclesiastique.'[2]

The official attitude of the Roman Church to Holy Scripture may be briefly defined by reference to two authoritative sources.

The Holy Oecumenical and General Synod of Trent . . . having this aim always before its eyes, that errors may be removed and the purity of the Gospel be preserved in the Church, which was before promised in the Holy Scriptures and which our Lord Jesus Christ the Son of God first published by his own mouth and then commanded to be preached to every creature as the source of all saving truth and of discipline of conduct; and perceiving that this truth and this discipline are contained in written books and in unwritten traditions, which were received by the Apostles from the lips of Christ himself, or by the same Apostles, at the dictation of the Holy Spirit, were handed on and have come down to us; following the example of the orthodox fathers, this Synod

[1] *Spirit of Catholicism*, p. 258 ff.
[2] *Evangile selon Saint Jean*, Introduction.

receives and venerates, with equal pious affection and reverence, all the books of the New and Old Testaments, since one God is the author of both, together with the said traditions, as well as those pertaining to faith as those pertaining to morals, as having been given either from the lips of Christ or by the Holy Spirit and preserved in the Catholic Church by a continuous succession.

That this decree of the Council of Trent (8 April 1546)[1] is to be understood still in the most uncompromising way is made clear, for instance, by the Encyclical *Providentissimus Deus* of Leo XIII (1893) in which it is written:

authority

> All the books and the whole of each book which the Church receives as sacred and canonical were written at the dictation of the Holy Spirit; and so far is it from being possible that any error can co-exist with divine inspiration that not only does the latter in itself exclude all error, but excludes and rejects it with the same necessity as attaches to the impossibility that God Himself, who is the supreme truth, should be the author of any error whatsoever.

Divine inspiration is thus regarded as inevitably exclusive of all error. It is assumed that, when God uses human writers to convey truth, he must of necessity take such steps as are necessary to overrule the normal human tendency to make mistakes. This is evidently part of what 'at the dictation of the Holy Spirit' is taken to mean. At first sight, therefore, the Roman view of

[1] H. Bettenson, *Documents of the Christian Church*, p. 365 (79-83).

Scripture appears to be unqualified literalism; and to some extent this is true, especially in as much as Roman expositors often seem as reluctant to reckon with the full import and to accept the method of modern biblical scholarship as the Conservative Evangelical authors of the *New Bible Commentary*.

Yet the Roman Catholic doctrine of the authority of Scripture differs very considerably from that of the Conservative Evangelicals, since the Roman Catholic would declare in a way which would be quite alien to such a Protestant that the Church is prior to Scripture, and therefore to be regarded as its creator, guardian, interpreter, its owner. The claim that the Scriptures have been handed over to the Church by God, and that the Church is, therefore, the owner and trustee of the Scriptures, is quite explicitly made in the *Catholic Commentary on Holy Scripture*:

> We must not, however, imagine Scripture and Tradition to be like two distinct reservoirs receiving the waters of divine truth from distinct and separate springs. There is in a sense but one source of revealed truth, viz. divine Tradition, by which is meant the body of truth handed down from the Apostles through the ages and contained in the doctrine, teaching and practice of the Catholic Church. Yet since a large and important part of that revelation was committed to writing both before and after the time of Christ, the Church is accustomed to speak of two sources of revelation, oral Tradition and Scripture. The peculiar character and importance of Scripture—the written part of this Tradition—derives solely from the fact that it is the inspired word of God. . . . The two streams of oral Tradition and Scrip-

B

ture happily mix, for in the living *magisterium* of the
Church these are living waters springing up unto life
everlasting. It is the Church, the holder of Tradition,
that gives life to the dead letter of Scripture.[1]

There is a certain truth in this position which non-
Romanists have been too reluctant to recognize. It is
impossible to deny that the Bible is the Church's book,
that it took its rise from within the Church's life. It was
the Church which recognized the canon of Scripture;
and it is within the life of the Church that the Bible is
to be read, studied, understood and expounded. This is
not to deny that the Bible may be read by many who
would not call themselves believers in any precise sense
of the word; but it is to claim that unless the Bible is
known and examined within the context of God's
saving purpose as recognized, accepted, and shared
within the life of the Church, the real clue to its meaning is obscured. Nor is there any reason to dispute the
claim that the Church is the guardian and expositor of
Scripture. The fellowship of the Spirit is the essential
context of biblical study of whatever kind. But every-
thing depends upon two issues. How is the Church to
be understood? What are its boundaries? The Roman
Church would claim that only within its tightly defined
borders can the Bible be guarded, understood, and expounded. This, to many Protestants, seems typical of
the way in which the Roman Church often imposes a
fatal qualification upon a valuable principle by making
titanic and sectarian claims for itself. To declare that

[1] W. Leonard and B. Orchard in *A Catholic Commentary on
Holy Scripture*, para. 1, p. 1. Cf. paras. 7a-8a, p. 8 ff.

the Bible and the Church belong together is one thing: to claim the Bible as the possession of the Roman Church is another.

There is, moreover, another and even more important issue to be faced. If the Bible and the Church belong together, as Protestants with the important qualifications just mentioned would agree, what is the relation of the one to the other? The Roman Church, as has been noted already, conceives itself as imparting authority to the Scriptures. To some extent, this is bound up with the assertion that the Bible is the product of the Church. Historically, the point is valid enough; but historical priority neither implies nor imparts spiritual priority. The Church created, accepted, preserved the words of Scripture; but it did not create the Word: indeed, the Word created the Church. Moreover, since the Church derives from the Word, and not the Word from the Church, it is by the Word that the faithfulness and the obedience of the Church must be judged. This is not the place at which to develop the argument that it is precisely the refusal of the Roman Church to admit that the Church can err and come under the judgment of the Word which seems to Protestant Christians one of its most flagrant errors; but the fact needs to be mentioned to indicate how impossible it is for Protestants to speak of the Church possessing the Word as if it stood over and not under it, as if it judged and were not judged by it: one of the fundamental differences between the Roman Catholics and the Protestants is exactly this issue of the relative priority of the Word and the Church.

No statement of Protestant conviction on this point is clearer than Luther's comment on Galatians 1.9 ('As we have said before, so now I say again, If any man is preaching to you a gospel contrary to that which you received, let him be accursed'):

> This sentence of Paul ought to admonish us, that so many as think the Pope to be the judge of the Scripture are accursed. Which thing the popish schoolmen have wickedly taught, standing upon this ground: the Church hath allowed four Gospels only: therefore there are but four: for if it had allowed more, there had been more. Now seeing the Church might receive and allow such and so many gospels as it would, therefore the Church is above the Gospel. A goodly argument forsooth. I approve the Scripture, ergo, I am above the Scripture. John Baptist acknowledgeth and confesseth Christ, and pointeth to him with his finger, therefore he is above Christ. The Church approveth the Christian faith and doctrine, therefore the Church is above them. For the overthrowing of this their wicked and blasphemous doctrine, thou hast here a plain text like a thunderbolt, wherein *Paul* subjecteth both himself and an angel from heaven, and doctors upon earth, and all other teachers and masters whatsoever under the authority of Scripture. For they ought not to be masters, judges, or arbiters, but only witnesses, disciples, and confessors of the Scripture, whether it be the Pope, *Luther, Augustine, Paul,* or an Angel from heaven. Neither ought any doctrine to be taught or heard in the Church, besides the pure word of God; that is to say, the holy Scripture. Otherwise, accursed be both teachers and hearers, together with their doctrine.[1]

[1] Luther's *Commentary on Galatians, ad loc.,* trans. 1575.

The Protestant, however, has a further difficulty with the Romanist attitude to Scripture. It is not only that Rome derives the authority of Scripture from that of the Church, but also that alongside Scripture it sets tradition.

The Council of Trent declared that the saving truth and discipline of conduct which Christ preached to the Apostles 'are contained in written books and in unwritten traditions, which were received by the Apostles from the lips of Christ himself, or, by the same Apostles, at the dictation of the Holy Spirit'. It also declared that it received and venerated 'with equal affection of piety and reverence all the books of the Old and of the New Testament, seeing that one God is the author of both, as also the said traditions, as having been dictated, either by Christ's own word of mouth, or by the Holy Ghost'. The Council anathematizes any who do not receive as sacred and canonical the Scriptures as they have been used in the Catholic Church and 'knowingly and deliberately contemn the traditions aforesaid'. It is further decreed that 'no one . . . shall . . . presume to interpret the said sacred Scripture contrary to that sense which holy mother Church whose it is to judge of the true sense and interpretation of the holy Scriptures, hath held and doth hold'.[1]

Thus the Roman Church believes that apart from what was written in the canonical Scriptures there was handed down through the Apostles an oral tradition which is supplementary to the written. Such texts as John 21.25 ('And there are also many other things

[1] Council of Trent, session iv.

which Jesus did; every one of them to be written, I
suppose that even the world itself could not contain the
books that would be written') and Acts 1.3 ('To them he
presented himself alive after his passion by many
proofs, appearing to them during forty days, and speaking of the Kingdom of God') are held to justify this
belief. But one must agree with Principal Cunliffe-Jones
that there is no shred of evidence for the existence 'of
a substantial body of doctrine which goes back to the
Apostolic tradition itself and has been preserved during
the centuries with a gradual unfolding of some of its
contents'.[1]

Whatever the origin of this tradition, however, it
now stands in Romanist thought alongside Scripture as
an independent authority. When this is understood in
the light of such teaching as J. H. Newman's on the
development of Christian doctrine, or Karl Adam's conception of Christianity as an organic unity which
grows, it is possible for *any* new doctrine to be presented as apostolic, since the Church, the guardian and
interpreter of tradition, has declared that it is so.
Giovanni Miegge's recent study of mariology is one
sustained piece of evidence of the way in which what
is unknown to Scripture and to Christian antiquity can
be presented as of saving faith by the declaration that
the Church transmits it as part of the original revelation. Of the many examples of which this occurs in
Miegge's book one may be taken, concerning the pro-
mulgation of the dogma of the Assumption of the

[1] H. Cunliffe-Jones, *The Authority of the Biblical Revelation*,
p. 72.

Virgin Mary. Pope Benedict XIV is quoted as declaring that 'the Assumption of the blessed Virgin is not an article of faith. . . . The texts of Scripture that are customarily adduced in its support can be interpreted otherwise and tradition is not enough to elevate this doctrine to the rank of articles of faith.' That was in the eighteenth century; but in 1950 Pope Pius XII's Bull *Munificentissimus Deus*, in which the dogma of the Assumption was defined, asserts that 'the Authority of the Church infallibly fulfils its mandate to conserve the integrity and purity of the revealed truth for all time, and to transmit it without adding to it or taking from it'; 'therefore from the universal consensus of the Church may be drawn a sure and certain argument for affirming the Assumption. It is a truth revealed by God.'[1] This, as Miegge observes, is simply saying that, since authority has been given to it to conserve the truth, whatever the Church proclaims must be said to be in accord with the deposit of faith. It is impossible not to agree with C. J. Cadoux's blunt remark that the doctrine of tradition as defined by the Council of Trent and since held by the Roman Church is 'simply an extraordinary clever device for vindicating Roman ordinances against the charge of novelty'.[2]

Why, it may be asked, does the Roman Church set such store upon a belief which can be attacked on historical and scriptural grounds? The answer is that suggested by Professor J. K. S. Reid: that in Roman theology it is assumed that Christianity must be a

[1] G. Miegge, *The Virgin Mary*, pp. 99 ff.
[2] C. J. Cadoux, *Catholicism and Christianity*, p. 297.

system of such a kind that on any point of faith or morals alike the inquiring believer may be told what to accept and believe in order to be saved. The Scriptures do not provide such a system; nor is it their purpose to do so. It is their purpose to witness to Christ that men may believe (John 20.31). It is to make good this lack of system that the tradition of the Church is used. Thus it becomes possible for the Roman Church to argue that the way it does things is on an equality with the gospel tradition, because the Church has Christ and is itself divine. 'At this point, it is to be feared, all conversation between the unreformed and the reformed churches comes to an abrupt end. So long as the Roman church shelters from the Bible behind its own developing tradition, it is unable to listen to the living voice that comes through Scripture. It can no doubt have long and even edifying monologues with itself, but in the last resort it rests in a refusal to let itself be told something from outside itself'.[1]

2   *Calvin's Teaching*

As far as Reformation theology is concerned, we may take John Calvin as a convenient illustration; and we may do so with the more confidence since he became the exemplar of Protestant thought in many areas and for a great length of time.

Calvin argued strongly against the view that the Church gives authority to the Bible, that on her nod

[1] J. K. S. Reid, *The Authority of Scripture*, p. 141.

its authority depends. 'While the Church receives and gives its seal of approval to the Scriptures, it does not thereby render authentic what was otherwise doubtful or controversial. But because the Church recognizes Scripture to be the truth of its own God, as a pious duty it unhesitatingly venerates Scripture.'[1]

But if the Scriptures are not to be accepted on the authority of the Church, how are we to be persuaded that they come from God? To this question Calvin gives the answer that it is much the same question, how shall we learn to distinguish between light and darkness, white and black, and sweet and bitter? Scripture bears upon its face clear evidence of its truth, as white and black do of their colour, and sweet and bitter of their taste.

The highest proof of Scripture is uniformly taken from him whose word it is. Indeed, if we bring those who speak against Scripture to acknowledge that 'the volume of Sacred Scripture very far surpasses all other writings', it would not at all follow that ' we shall forthwith implant the certainty which faith requires in their hearts'. The reason for this is that religion does not rest, as is often supposed, on reason: the testimony of the Spirit is superior to reason.

As God alone is a fit witness of himself in his Word, so also the Word will not find acceptance in men's hearts before it is sealed by the inward testimony of the Spirit. The same Spirit, therefore, who has spoken by the mouth of the prophets must penetrate into our hearts, to persuade us that they faith-

[1] *Institutes* I vii 2, trans. F. L. Battles (SCM Press).

fully proclaimed what has been divinely commanded.[1]

Those whom the Holy Spirit has inwardly taught
truly rest upon Scripture, and Scripture indeed is self-
authenticated; hence, it is not right to subject it to
proof or reasoning. And the certainty it deserves with
us it attains by the testimony of the Spirit. . . .
Illumined by his power, we believe, neither by our
own nor by anyone else's judgment, that Scripture
is from God; but . . . we affirm with utter certainty
. . . that it has flowed to us from the very mouth of
God by the ministry of men. We seek no proofs, no
marks of genuineness on which our judgment may
lean; but we subject our judgment and wit to it as to
a thing far beyond any guesswork. This we do . . .
not like those miserable men who habitually bind
over their minds to the thraldom superstitution; but
we feel that the undoubted power of his divine
majesty lives and breaths there.[2]

Calvin does not deny that there are several secondary
ways in which the Scriptures may be brought home to
us; and he is prepared to give full weight to the
evidential value of the dignity, truth and simplicity of
Scripture, and to the way in which its several parts
cohere. In a style which would not be nearly as convincing today, he holds that the miracles and fulfilled
predictions in the Bible lead men to belief. But when
full weight has been given to these considerations,
Calvin teaches that none of them, nor all of them
together, can produce firm faith in the Scriptures, until
the heavenly Father manifests his presence in it, and
thereby secures implicit reverence for it. 'Scripture will

[1] *Institutes* I vi 4.   [2] *Institutes* I vii 5.

ultimately suffice for a saving knowledge of God only when its certainty is founded upon the inward persuasion of the Holy Spirit.'[1]

Further exposition of what Calvin believed about the work of the Holy Spirit in authenticating the word of God in Scripture is given in his exposition of what St Paul says about the letter which 'killeth' and the Spirit which 'giveth life', and the law 'written on the hearts of believers through the ministration of the Spirit' (II Corinthians 3.6 ff.) :

> The Word itself is not quite certain for us unless it be confirmed by the testimony of the Spirit. . . . For the Lord has joined together the certainty of his Word and of his Spirit so that the perfect religion of the Word may abide in our minds when the Spirit, who causes us to contemplate God's face, shines; and that we may in turn embrace the Spirit with no fear of being deceived when we recognize him in his own image, namely, in the Word.[2]

While there are thoughts and phrases in his writings which could easily petrify into a literalist understanding of the Bible, the whole emphasis of his thinking is less rigid and more spiritual. At times his conviction that we cannot know the saving power of the Gospel without becoming pupils of Scripture[3] almost drives him to speaking of the Scriptures as 'God's own voice', 'dictated by the Holy Spirit', and of writers of Scripture as 'sure and genuine scribes of the Holy Spirit'.[4] But we have to note as equally significant the light hearted in-

[1] *Institutes* I viii 13.   [2] *Institutes* I ix 3.
[3] *Institutes* I vi 2.   [4] *Institutes* I vii 1, IV viii 5, 9.

difference with which Calvin treated trifling discrepancies in the sacred narrative. While Calvin can say on the one hand that 'Every word which may have issued forth from God is to be received with implicit authority, and no countenance given to that abominable practice of refusing to receive a doctrine, unless it can be supported by two or three texts of Scripture',[1] he can be surprisingly 'modern' in some of his opinions. Since this is an aspect of Calvin's thought which is either unknown or doubted, some detailed evidence may be given here, from which it will become perfectly clear that he was no literalist, as that term is normally understood.

Calvin cast doubt upon the authenticity of II Peter, James, and Jude. Of a notorious *crux interpretum*, Matthew 28.9, he writes, 'I confess that I do not know how the name of Jeremiah comes to be here, and I do not worry much about it'.[2] In the introduction to his commentary on Joshua, he dismisses the problem of authorship with the remark that we need not hesitate 'to pass over a matter which we are unable to determine, or the knowledge of which is not very necessary, while we are in no doubt as to the essential point—that the doctrine herein contained was dictated by the Holy Spirit for our use, and confers benefits of ordinary kind on those who attentively peruse it'. Nor did Calvin suppose that all the Psalms were written by David. Of Psalms 44 and 129 he says that they are probably of the Maccabean period; and of Psalm 47 that it came either from the reign of Ahaz or the time of Jehoshaphat or Asa. 'I do not think it is probable that David was its author', he writes of

[1] *Comm.*, Ps. 62.11.   [2] *Comm., ad loc.*

Psalm 18; 'because when he bewails the persecutions which he suffered in the time of Saul, it is usual with him to interpose some particular reference to himself. My opinion, then, rather is, that this form of prayer was composed for all the godly by some prophet, either when the Jews were captive in Babylon, or when Antiochus Epiphanes exercised towards them most relentless cruelty.' The same kind of critical judgment is brought to bear upon the account of the creation of the world, given in the opening chapters of Genesis. On Genesis 1.6, which records the creation of the firmament, Calvin makes this comment: 'he who would learn astronomy and other recondite arts, let him go elsewhere'. Of Genesis 1.16, which has to do with the making of the greater and lesser lights and the stars, he says: 'Moses wrote in a popular style things which without instruction, all ordinary persons, endued with common sense, are able to understand; but astronomers investigate with great labour whatever the sagacity of the human mind can comprehend. . . . Had he spoken of things generally unknown, the uneducated might have pleaded the excuse that such subjects were beyond their capacity.' If only Victorian Christians had grasped what Calvin had understood three centuries earlier, theologians and scientists might have been saved many wordy and often fruitless battles!

If Calvin could see that the biblical writers did not set out to provide scientific knowledge, he was also cautious in judging whether certain 'prophecies' in the Old Testament were 'fulfilled' in the New. Of Jeremiah 31.15 ('A voice is heard in Ramah,' quoted at Matthew

2.18 in connexion with the massacre of the Holy Inno-
cents), Calvin's comment is: 'This passage is quoted by
Matthew, where he gives an account of the infants
under two years old, who had been slain at the com-
mand of Herod: then he says, that this prophecy was
fulfilled, even that Rachel again wept for her children.
But the explanation of this is attended with no difficulty; for Matthew meant no other than that the same
thing happened at the coming of Christ as had taken
place before, when the whole country was reduced to
desolation.' Of Psalm 126.1, which speaks of the Lord
turning again the captivity of Zion, Calvin somewhat
tartly remarks that 'it is unnatural and forced to suppose, with some expositors, that this is a prediction of
what was to come'—which it would be necessary to do
in order to uphold the Davidic authorship of the Psalm.
'For my part, I have no doubt that the Psalm was composed upon the return of the Jewish people from the
Babylonian captivity.'

On the one hand, therefore, Calvin did not scruple to
describe the Bible as 'such written proof of the heavenly
doctrine, that it should neither perish through forgetful-
ness nor vanish through error nor be corrupted by the
audacity of men',[1] with the result that for many of his
disciples 'truth came to be regarded as static and fixed,
capable of being put into the pages of a book and
handed down from generation to generation'.[2] On the
other hand, Calvin was evidently not tied to a literalist
view of Scripture;[3] and for all his veneration of the letter

[1] *Institutes*, I vi 3.
[2] A. Dakin, *Calvanism*, p. 190.   [3] *Institutes*, I vii 5.

of Scripture, he never regarded the Bible as a merely external standard of truth. As the Westminster Confession declares (article 5): 'Full persuasion and assurance of the infallible truth and divine authority (of the Scriptures) is from the inward work of the Holy Spirit, bearing witness by and with the Word in our hearts.'

It may, therefore, be truly said that for Calvin 'between the Word of God *simpliciter* and conviction by the Word of God lies the work of the Holy Spirit'. The recognition of the Word of God as authoritative is 'not made independently of what is recognized, but consists rather in an apprehension of the mind, aroused by the Holy Spirit, of the truth of what is said and acceptance of it by the heart; the authority of the Scriptures derives from the Christ to whom it is their office to attest'. Yet 'the seat of their authority is outside themselves, in him to whom they are the attestation. Such authority as the Holy Scriptures possess is therefore a derivative and conceded authority, imparted to them by him to whom they witness'.[1] While, therefore, Calvin makes much of the objectivity of the written Word of God, he nevertheless lays much stress on the inward testimony of the Spirit. It is to Charles Wesley that we owe the best short statement of this aspect of Calvin's teaching:

> Come, Holy Ghost, for moved by Thee,
>   The Prophets wrote and spoke;
> Unlock the truth, Thyself the key,
>   Unseal the sacred book.[2]

[1] J. K. S. Reid, *The Authority of Scripture*, pp. 47, 54.
[2] Methodist *Hymn Book* (Britain) 305, *Hymnal* (USA) 175.

But, it may be objected, is not this to argue in a circle? Is all that Calvin has said simply that the Holy Spirit has inspired the Holy Scriptures and that he illuminates the minds of the readers to perceive the meaning of what he originally inspired? Fundamentally this is what he has to say; but before it can be dismissed as mere circular argument, the testimony of the Bible itself needs to be borne in mind.

The New Testament maintains that spiritual things are spiritually discerned (I Corinthians 2.14). It could well be argued that what St Paul says about faith in Christ is in essential respects similar to what here is said about perceiving the meaning of Scripture. In I Corinthians 12 St Paul lists the gifts of the spirit (vv. 4-11); and wisdom and faith are among those enumerated. This, however, is preceded (vv. 1-3) by an attempt to correct some wrong beliefs about spiritual gifts. Evidently some had supposed that merely to be able to utter in tongues was a sufficient sign of having received the Spirit; but the Apostle fastens attention on the content of the utterance. If the supposedly spirit-possessed person declares 'Jesus is accursed', it is clearly not God's Spirit who has inspired him; and if anyone is led to declare 'Jesus is Lord', it can only have been the Holy Spirit who made the statement possible. To make such a confession of faith does not come at the end of some line of argument or chain of reflection, though no doubt these may have their right and necessary part in the total experience of conversion and coming to faith. The *essence* of that experience is a moment of illumination, perception and commitment which is impossible without the work of the Holy Spirit (see Matthew 16.17). Similarly, Calvin may argue that to perceive the real quality of the Holy Scriptures and at any particular point to grasp its meaning is quite beyond the unaided powers of human reason. We have seen that he took no obscurantist delight in stifling the process of human reason in settling the meaning of the Bible either in general or at particular points, any more than St Paul sought to make faith in Christ an irrational experience; but as that is not to be understood merely in rational terms and not without dependence upon the Spirit, so believing insight into the meaning of the Bible is not given unless the Holy Spirit illuminates the mind of the reader. It is thus that the Scriptures have authority with men.

Calvin, however, does more than declare and safe-guard the Spirit's witness to the truth of what he him-self has inspired. He deals theologically with a fact of experience which, as we shall see, Liberal Protestantism emphasized without being able to account for with any deep theological seriousness. The Bible 'finds' people. Just as David is confronted with a Nathan (II Samuel 12.7 ff.), who strips away from him his moral indigna-tion against the meanness of some landowner's be-haviour towards a neighbouring crofter, and brings home to him the meaning of his own sin against Uriah with 'Thou art the man', so the Holy Scriptures are used by the Holy Spirit to speak to men and women, whether to rebuke or uplift. At such moments, it is as if the historical, written words 'leap out of the page' at the reader. To use P. T. Forsyth's phrase to describe the same experience, 'the wire glows with the current'. The reader is personally addressed. He knows the inner witness of the Spirit as the things of God are declared to him; and the Scriptures bear authority, for God has spoken through them.

3   *The 'Modern' Approach*

It is not so easy to deal with what the 'modern' approach to the Bible assumes to be the authority of Scripture, since there is no widely accepted statement of its position on this issue of comparable clarity and power as is to be found in Calvin's *Institutes*. But a brief description of its fundamental attitudes to biblical studies provides a sufficient clue as to the way the Bible is thought to bring itself home to men's hearts and minds.[1]

There is no need to deal here with the history of the critical method, save to remark that, while the critical study of the Bible began in the latter half of the eighteenth century and was worked with increasing confidence during the nineteenth and so far into the twentieth centuries, it had no doubt some roots in the Renaissance and in the critical attitude of mind then developed and encouraged. In the main this approach to the study of the Bible treats the Scriptures very much as it would any other ancient document; and it has developed two distinct, though related, studies. One, usually called 'lower' criticism, deals with such matters

[1] A much fuller treatment of this theme is provided by James D. Smart, *The Interpretation of Scripture*.

as the restoration of the text through the comparison of manuscripts and ancient versions: it is much concerned with the detection of scribal errors. It seeks to obtain and provide as reliable a text of the Scriptures as possible. The so-called 'higher' criticism, on the other hand, examines such questions as authorship, date, sources and kindred matters; and any modern work on the Pentateuch or the Synoptic Gospels affords quick illustration of this method and its results.

This method of biblical study rests on the insight that, whatever may be the religious or divine aspect of the Scriptures, they have a human origin and history, which is capable of examination by scholarly methods. To recognize this does not necessarily evacuate the Scriptures of their divine meaning. But it does imply that this cannot be understood as it was previously. Once the Bible is looked at in this critical way, it becomes obvious that the human factor in its composition involves the fact (or, at the very least, the possibility) of error. Infallibility, at any rate as once understood, is no longer credible.

Critics of this method often vilify those who follow it because the results of their studies have not been unanimous or 'assured'; but, while the charge has to be admitted to a considerable extent, it must be said that to ask for complete unanimity and absolutely assured results is to expect from this method more than it can supply and to judge it by standards which are not relevant. The clear-cut decisions of the literalists are impossible in literary criticism, for judgments will inevitably differ, and equally competent scholars will reach different conclusions as to the meaning of the same body of facts, as is shown, for example, by the discussion of the authorship of the Fourth Gospel. Those who follow the critical method expect to advance their studies by discussion, by sifting evidence, by testing hypotheses, by looking at the first three Gospels side by side, and by asking out of what sort of situation and necessity the Gospels came to be written. Their under-standing of their method prevents them from expecting of it what it cannot provide, and their readiness to con-sider fresh evidence precludes them from regarding any issue as closed; and perhaps it is here even more than anywhere else that the difference between this attitude to biblical studies and that of its opponents is most clearly to be seen.

By one of the most unfortunate mischances of history, the critical study of the Bible fell under the spell of two dominating ideas, neither of which is at all necessarily connected with it: the doctrine of the uni-versal reign of law and that of biological evolution. As to the former, Harnack's famous dictum provides suffi-cient evidence: 'we are firmly convinced that what happens in space and time is subject to the general laws of motion, and that in this sense, as an interruption of the order of nature, there can be no such thing as miracles'.[1] The Bible is thus judged by the general scien-tific view of the time. As to the latter, we may recall Bousset's remark to the effect that Christianity is no more than 'the highest point which religious develop-ment has reached'. Since the evolutionary view of life

[1] *What Is Christianity?* p. 28.

hates finality, any notion of the finality of the Christian religion was really abandoned. The whole issue is thus summed up by T. W. Manson in a much-quoted essay: 'the attempt of Liberalism to deal with the history of biblical religion was vitiated by its dogmatic presuppositions. Having taken up its axioms, which were at variance with the fundamental ideas of the Bible, there was no way of carrying the business through which did not involve picking and choosing among the biblical material on a scale and with an arbitrariness quite impossible to justify'.[1] This, however, does not mean that the critical method should be jettisoned; rather, 'we must retrace our steps to the point where Liberalism went off the track, and having reached that point, we must go forward not backward'.[2]

It should be honestly recognized that this is not as easily done as said, for biblical scholarship has shown itself remarkably prone to follow passing fashions, sometimes swinging from one extreme to another, with one generation accusing its predecessor of error while falling into a similar fault. 'It is easy to laugh at those who a couple of generations ago, saw in Jesus a good nineteenth-century liberal humanist with a simple faith in a paternal deity. It is less easy to see the joke when the Jesus of history is a twentieth-century existentialist.'[3] True as that is, however, critical scholarship is concerned to assert that a certain method of biblical

[1] *The Interpretation of the Bible*, ed. C. W. Dugmore, p. 102.
[2] *Ibid.*, p. 101.
[3] T. W. Manson in *The Background of the New Testament*, ed. W. D. Davies and D. Daube, p. 220.

study is right and should be followed 'wherever the argument leads'. Treating the Bible as any other book of antiquity, it seeks to discover the facts about the human history of the Scriptures, and it argues that what we know of that history must have its effect upon the way in which we estimate the resultant writings. No matter how incautious some theories advanced by certain scholars may be nor how shocking their consequences may appear to those who do not recognize that in all sorts of ways an historical religion is vulnerable from the historian's side, this method of study cannot be dismissed out of hand because of the apparent aberrations of some of its followers, whose work must in any case be judged by the austere standards of this very method itself. However far we travel from this or that theory of the composition of the Pentateuch or of the Synoptic Gospels, it is incredible that we should ever turn our backs on this method of biblical study with its insistent demand that what we say about the biblical documents should accord with normally accepted standards of evidence.

We must also remember that it is becoming more and more recognized by the exponents of the critical method that the Bible provides its own criterion of interpretation, and that it is mistaken to seek to expound its truth by standards such as a 'steel-and-concrete' view of the laws of nature, the latest mode of existentialist philosophy, or any other yardstick whatsoever, since these are external to it and therefore irrelevant. Just as there has been a fresh awarenss of the Bible's unity (as distinct from its diversity, which it was fashionable to emphasize about fifty years ago), so there has been an increasing recognition of the fact that the very source of this unity provides the category by which the Bible is to be understood. The Bible is seen to tell the story of the redemption of the world through the gracious activity of the Creator, a redemption which reaches its climax in the victory of Jesus Christ and the continuance of his ministry in the Church. The record of this activity in the Bible is seen to be part of the objective element in revelation; and it stands, no matter what human flaws we may detect in the record. Nor is it one whit lessened in value because not every word of Scripture can necessarily be proved to bear witness to some aspect of the divine activity. The preacher may not see how to preach Christ from the text about Og the King of Bashan and his bedstead of iron (Deuteronomy 3.11); but his incapacity at that point does not offer any real obstacle to believing that the Bible is a book about the work of God's redeeming grace, and that it is, as Luther said, the crib in which Christ is laid.

It has been necessary to take this brief glance at the presuppositions and development of the critical study of the Bible before asking what sort of views about the authority of the Bible are characteristic of it. What appears to have happened is that at the beginning of this period there was a natural revolt against the biblical scholasticism of the day, which, being largely a hardened, narrowed, not to say soured, version of Calvin's theology, tended more and more to think of the Bible as a merely external authority. It was as necessary as it was natural that men should take the liberty to look at the Bible as an ordinary book, and work at it to discover afresh for themselves what was in it, to set it free from all its theological framework, and to let it 'find' them as it would. What has been said earlier in this book about a view of the inspiration of the Bible in terms of religious experience is closely akin to what falls to be said now about the view of biblical authority which goes naturally with it. Such a phrase as 'the authority of religious genius' is characteristic of this way of seeing the matter; the human authors of Scripture were looked upon as experts in the knowledge of God, and it was held that they had through their personal inspiration apprehended fresh and creative ideas which have a cogent persuasiveness. Thus it was that the Bible was regarded as the record of their experience and insight and was considered to have the sort of authority which belongs to a book which not only records but through recording kindles in others such normative religious experience. 'The function of authority is to secure assent to truth,' and 'the measure of any authority which the Bible may possess lies in its direct religious value, open to discovery in experience; and . . . this value in turn will be related to the experience out of which the Scriptures came'.[1]

It does not need to be emphasized that such an understanding of biblical authority gives us a considerable part of the truth. The Bible must for ever remain external to us, unless at some moment and in some way we are enabled to apprehend what it conveys. But to

[1] C. H. Dodd, *The Authority of the Bible*, 1928 ed., p. ix.

base the authority of the Bible on the religious experience of its human authors, and on the ability of the record of that experience to rekindle a like experience in the heart of the reader, is surely to exalt internal authority at the expense of any external standard of authority at all. As Dr Hebert well says:

> The Hebrew prophets did indeed seek God and find him in intense religious experience; but it was not the case that this experience formed the basis of their faith. The prophets belonged to a tradition, which they had learned from their fathers in the faith; and the basis of that faith was, according to their own account, that the Lord God had by His own act chosen Israel to a position of special privilege. . . . With one accord prophets and psalmists refer back to . . . events of the remote past, as the decisive points at which God had revealed himself.[1]

While this is said of the Old Testament prophets in particular, it may equally well be said of the rest of the biblical writers. It is not religious experience which is authoritative, but the gracious activity of God as made known in his saving deeds in history. The norm of Christian truth is not within the reader of the Scriptures, any more than it is in their human authors. Scripture is the record of God's redeeming activity; and it derives its authority from him whose deeds it records.

As the critical study of the Bible has proceeded from its earlier historicism to its current interest in *heilsgeschichte* ('saving-history'), it has come more and more to assume, rather than to express in so many words,

[1] A. G. Hebert, *The Authority of the Old Testament*, pp. 34 ff.

that the Scriptures derive a 'conceded' authority as recording God's redemptive activity, and that this
authority is exercised as their message awakens conviction in those who read them. The Christian would claim
that it is the Holy Spirit who awakens this conviction.
What H. Wheeler Robinson wrote towards the end of
Inspiration and Revelation in the Old Testament is true
of the Bible as a whole. He argues that the colloquy of
God with the prophet carried its own authority with it,
so that it needed no 'external testimony, necessarily
lower than its source and nature as divine truth'.
Although what the biblical writers have to communi-
cate to us must of necessity come to us through the
Bible and the Church, 'the way in which the "inspired"
were convinced that the very truth of God had come to
them is still the way in which this conviction becomes
ours. Without tradition we could not attain knowledge,
but without personal conviction that knowledge could
not be assimilated as revelation.' The Bible, like the
witness of the Church, is an important link in the chain
'which hangs from nothing less than God Himself, and
becomes visible to us only at the point at which he
chooses to enter our consciousness'.[1]

[1] *Op. cit.*, p. 274 f.

III

'FUNDAMENTALISM'

1 *Are Conservative Evangelicals Literalists?*

'FUNDAMENTALISM' IS A question-begging term, which appears to bear two meanings. It is often said that the word describes not literalism, i.e. belief that every word in the Bible is literally true, but a concern for the fundamentals of the Christian faith.[1] The Bible is believed to deliver certain doctrines, which it is orthodox to believe because they are in the Bible. As a rule these doctrines are held to include the inerrancy of Scripture, a particular doctrine of the Second Advent of our Lord, a highly individualistic doctrine of the Holy Spirit, a weighty emphasis on the substitutionary aspect of the Atonement, while it has very little to say about the Church. It is doubtful whether this can be regarded as a balanced account of New Testament teaching; and there have been those who have not scrupled to describe it as heretical, sectarian and exclusive.[2]

It is in a somewhat different sense, however, that the word 'fundamentalism' is normally used in connection with the Bible. In this context it is usually taken to mean (rightly or wrongly) 'literalism', as describing the

[1] A. G. Hebert, *Fundamentalism and the Church of God,* pp. 9-10 and 17-19.
[2] See A. M. Ramsey, now Archbishop of Canterbury, in *The Bishoprick* (Feb. 1956), p. 25.

attitude of those who believe that the Bible is a book
'written by God through thirty secretaries'. Most
Conservative Evangelicals reject this use of the
word 'fundamentalist' and regard it as something of
a libel; there is much justice in their claim. Among
Conservative Evangelicals there has been a somewhat
more open attitude to critical methods than could be
thought possible fifty years ago; and, especially in the
field of 'lower' criticism, though by no means only
there, conservative scholars have done outstanding
work. Yet it remains true that the equation of fundamentalism with literalism was accurate not so very long
ago; and, apart from the scholars, literalism is still the
real conviction of many Conservative Evangelicals
today.

While it is true that there is a somewhat more open
attitude to critical methods than was the case fifty
years or so ago, there is still caution enough. The Mosaic
authorship of the Pentateuch is still asserted in the *New
Bible Commentary*;[1] and the commentator on the
Epistles to Timothy and Titus in that volume avoids the
question of St Paul's authorship on the ground that the
considerations involved are 'largely unprofitable and
simply create hesitation and misgiving'.[2] We may ask
whether this is an honest way of dealing with a matter
of truth; and this prevarication is typical of the caution
which betokens that the ghost of B. B. Warfield is still
vigilant and walks in many places. He, at least, believed

---

[1] *Op. cit.*, p. 75.ii, p. 106.i, p. 134.ii, p. 162.ii, p. 195.ii; but
see also p. 34.ii, where G. C. Aalders offers a somewhat different view.   [2] *Ibid.*, p. 1063.i.

that the biblical writers were so dealt with by the Holy
Spirit 'that their words became at one and the same time
the words of God, and thus, *in every sense and all alike,
infallible*'.[1] From this it is clear that the written Word is
authoritative; and a good many Conservative Evangelicals today write as if they wished this were true. The
written Word, truth 'inscripturated', has a special fas-
cination for them; and thus there arises what seems to
many to be the utmost reluctance to face what appear
to be the plain facts. There are those who are not tarred
with the same brush as Harnack and Wellhausen, who
do not treat the Bible with any off-handed arbitrariness,
who are nevertheless even more ill at ease with the Conservative Evangelicals simply because they appear to
hedge about the search for truth with dogmatic considerations. Indeed, it sometimes appears that Conservative Evangelicals will go with critical scholarship so far
as (and no further than) it permits them to go on treating the Bible as if none of this scholarship mattered at
all. It is at this point that we have to ask whether God
wishes us to pretend. If the Bible came into existence in
a certain way, ought we to treat it as if it had been
brought about in some other way?

'The Bible is none other than the voice of Him that
sitteth upon the throne. Every book of it, every chapter
of it, every verse of it, every word of it, every syllable
of it (where are we to stop?), every letter of it, is the
direct utterance of the Most High. The Bible is none
other than the Word of God, not some part of it more,
some part of it less, but all alike the utterance of him

[1] *Op. cit.*, p. 422 (italics mine).

that sitteth upon the throne, faultless, unerring, supreme.'[1] That is where Conservative Evangelicals once stood: and since that utterance in the mid-nineteenth century, while some reluctant concessions have been made to a less literalist attitude, the same fascinated awe for the written Word is still characteristic of their thinking. This is well exemplified in the article by G. W. Bromiley in the *New Bible Commentary* on the Authority of Scripture,[2] which may be taken as a representative, though not an official, statement of what Conservative Evangelicals nowadays hold to be the truth of this matter.

It is argued that if the Bible did not claim to be regarded as authoritative we should have no call to accept it as such; indeed, we need only accept it as authoritative 'in so far as the Bible requires it'. 'If the Bible stands before us as an authoritative Word of God, a Word which itself claims authority, then it is as such that we must reckon with it, receiving that Word and the authority of that Word, or resisting it.' Indeed; but the question is whether the Bible makes such a claim, and, if so, in what way; and it is as to 'in what way' that the discussion chiefly turns.

Dr Bromiley's article contains the assertion that the Bible itself claims authority for the written Word of Scripture; and he claims that in the New Testament, especially with reference to the Old Testament, this claim is indeed underwritten by our Lord himself. The evidence cited for this contention is that our Lord

[1] J. W. Burgon, *Inspiration and Interpretation* (1861), p. 89
[2] *Op. cit.*, pp. 15 ff.

answered the Tempter 'It is written', that on the Mount of Transfiguration he told his disciples that it is written of the Son of Man that he should suffer many things, that to the Jews he declared that the Scriptures 'testify of me', and that after the Resurrection he expounded to the disciples 'in all the Scriptures' the things concerning himself. This evidence, it is claimed, 'makes it quite plain that Jesus Himself accepted the inspiration and authority of the written Word, especially in so far as it gave prophetic witness to His own death and resurrection'. It is further claimed that verses like John 14.26 and 6.14 mean that he expected and promised a similar inspiration in the case of the apostolic testimony yet to be made.

The argument proceeds to assert that the apostles give equally clear testimony to the divine authority of the Bible. Paul's frequent quotation from the Old Testament is explained in the light of II Timothy 3.16 ('All Scripture is inspired by God and profitable for teaching, for reproof, for correction, and for training in righteousness.') II Peter 1.20, 21 and 3.16 are taken to imply that the New Testament writers were quite aware that they were adding to the corpus of authoritative Scripture.

More than all this, a great deal is made of the fact that our Lord does not question the connexion of Moses with the Law or the Davidic authorship of Psalm 110, and that the apostles accept all the main events of Old Testament history from Adam and the Fall to the crossing of the Red Sea, the Balaam incidents, the fall of Jericho, the deliverances under the Judges, the miracles of Elijah. All this evidence, taken together, is said to make it impossible to deny 'that, in the New Testament, belief in the authority of the Old does involve an acceptance of its historical as well as its religious and doctrinal truth'.

While Dr Bromily is anxious not to read more into this self-attestation of Scripture than is actually there, the evidence cited seems to be sufficient to warrant the assertion 'that the Bible does lay serious claim to divine origin, status and authority. It states clearly that its message is of God. It traces back its authorship through the human writings to the Holy Spirit. . . . It makes no artificial distinction between the inward content of the Word of God and its outward form.'[1]

2   *Dr Packer on Scriptural Authority*

The most vigorous and the ablest defence of Conservative Evangelicalism in recent years is *Fundamentalism and the Word of God*, by Dr J. I. Packer.[1] 'The general question which Christian students must face before ever they tackle any specific critical issues is this: should the principles governing our study of Scripture be drawn from Scripture itself, or not?' To that question, as it stands, there might be a more affirmative answer than Dr Packer would expect, since all devout scholars would wish their study of the Scriptures to be consistent with their nature, as they understand it. It could, however, be argued that the students he has in

[1] See also J. W. Wenham, *Our Lord's View of the Old Testament*.

mind might be in a better and stronger position to answer this question after they had become aware of what critical questions actually involve. At all events, Dr Packer does not regard this as a hard question to answer. 'Christian believers, who acknowledge the authority of Christ as Teacher in other matters, ought equally to acknowledge it in their approach to the Bible; they should receive the Scriptures as he did, accepting it to be divinely inspired and true and studying it as such. Those who pooh-pooh such an approach as obscurantist, unscientific and intellectually dishonest, should remember that they hereby stigmatize Jesus Christ, who taught his disciples this approach and thereby excluded any other.'[1] An earlier sentence makes plain the gravamen of Dr Packer's charge against those with whom he disagrees. 'They accept what they do accept, not simply because it is Scripture, but because it satisfies some further criterion of credibility which they have set up; so that even when they believe the right thing, in so far as they are consistent subjectivists they do so for the wrong reason.'[2]

But what is Scripture? This is the question which the critical method seeks to answer. It is relatively easy for Dr Packer to mock the critics for lack of 'assured results' and for relying too naïvely on popular hypotheses: the point is well made. It would be just as easy and just as irrelevant to make fun of the quite extraordinary variety of conclusions to which 'fundamentalists' come about the meaning of the divinely inspired Scripture. The real issue, however, is not whether

[1] *Ibid.*, p. 141.   [2] *Ibid.*, p. 140.

C

critical scholarship has had from time to time to shift its
ground, because some hypothesis was seen eventually
to be of limited usefulness or some other of wider application had come to light, but whether the critical
method itself is justified. Is it right, for instance, to
enquire what precisely are the documents which com-
prise the Bible? What is their history? Who composed
them and in what circumstances? Are there traces of
scribal emendations? How can similarities between,
say, the Gospels of Matthew and Luke best be explained? Do the normal canons of historical evidence
apply to holy documents? If these are legitimate questions, much depends on the answers we give, which
must inevitably be conditioned by the present state of
our knowledge: future discoveries may make us change
our minds about some critical issues. All our conclusions cannot be other than provisional, even though we
may think that some are much less likely to be over-
turned than others. At any given time we have to do the
best we can with whatever hypotheses best explain the
facts as we understand them. All this, however, assumes
that we may ask of sacred documents the same questions as about any other ancient literature, in which
case the first question any student of Scripture must
ask, be he Christian or agnostic, is, 'What is the nature
of these documents?' It may be that what is now
known about the human authors of Scripture, and of
the ways in which the Bible came into existence, make
a certain view of biblical inspiration and authority impossible. This is not at all to deny that they 'have
authority' and 'are inspired', though it is to say that

authority and inspiration have to be differently conceived than they are by Dr Packer.

The kernel of the argument in Dr Packer's book is that our Lord taught a particular view of the Old Testament and its authority; and since so much turns on this argument, it is necessary to examine it in some detail.

Jesus, says Dr Packer, 'did not hesitate to challenge and condemn, on his own authority, many accepted Jewish ideas which seemed to him false. But he never opposed his personal authority to that of the Old Testament. . . . The fact we have to face is that Jesus Christ, the Son of God incarnate, who claimed divine authority for all that he did and taught, both confirmed the absolute authority of the Old Testament for others and submitted himself unreservedly to it.'[1] Moreover, it is claimed that Jesus told his hearers that their eternal destiny depended on whether, having heard his words, they kept them; and Matthew 7.24 and John 12.48 are quoted in support of the contention.

But what does this mean? Is it consistent with the New Testament usage of 'faith' or with the doctrine of justification by faith to say that a man's eternal destiny depends on accepting words or a form of words? We accept a Saviour, not a rabbi. But how are we to understand 'absolute authority'? Naturally, God's Word has absolute authority; but in what sense God's Word and the Old Testament are related is precisely what Dr Packer has set out to prove. How are these words of Jesus to be taken as giving an overall authority to the Old Testament, and on what grounds are we to take

[1] *Ibid.*, p. 55.

them so? And what are we to understand by the idea
of Jesus submitting himself to the Old Testament? The
theological issues here are deep and very involved; but
if Dr Packer believes, as assuredly he does, that Jesus
was the Word Incarnate, in what sense does he understand him as able to submit himself to that partial
revelation of himself given in the Old Testament
(Hebrews 1.1, 2)?

Part of what this is intended to mean is drawn out in
a description of the way in which this submission is to
be observed. Dr Packer writes in words with which all
could agree of the way in which Jesus Christ met the
Tempter by words of Scripture, of the claim made in
controversy with the scribes and pharisees that he and
his disciples were in fact not breaking the sabbath but
keeping it as it was intended to be kept, and of the
importance of the Old Testament for the conception of
the messianic office which Jesus accepted and presented
to men. That Jesus 'ended a life of obedience to Scripture by dying in obedience to Scripture, looking to his
Father to raise him from death in fulfilment of Scripture', is one way of stating the truth. But it invites at
least two comments. (1) Why does Dr Packer speak of
'obedience to Scripture' instead of 'obedience to the
Father'? The latter seems a more accurate and a more
sensitive way of describing what is recorded in the
Gospels, especially in the agonized cry 'Thy will be
done', which is not somehow adequately translated into
'The Scripture be fulfilled'. (2) Even when it is agreed to
the full that Jesus saw his life, passion and triumph as a
fulfilment of Scripture, and that this is good evidence

of his attitude to Scripture, nothing has been said, still less proved, about the nature of the authority Scripture possesses. To say that 'he challenged current interpretations of Scripture, but shared and endorsed the accepted view of its nature and status as an authoritative utterance of God', even if accepted, tells us nothing precise about the meaning of 'authoritative'.

It is next argued that Christ's answer to the problem of scriptural authority can be summed up by saying that the Old Testament is to be accepted on the basis of his authority as the 'authoritative written utterance of God, abidingly true and trustworthy'. We are told that the teaching of Christ is to be taken together with the Old Testament, 'reading the old revelation as the presupposition of the new and the new as expounding and augmenting the old; in conjunction with Christ's teaching, the written word of the Old Testament retains its full divine authority'.[1] The foundation on which this rests is the conviction that if we accept Christ's authority at all, we commit ourselves to believe 'all that he taught—on his authority'. If we refuse to believe part of what he taught, we are in effect denying him to be Messiah—'on our own authority'. 'If we reject his attitude to the Old Testament, we are saying in effect that he founded Christianity on a fallacy. And if we say he was wrong here, we imply that he was wrong everywhere.' In this connexion Dr Packer quotes with approval these words of Professor Tasker: 'If he could be mistaken on matters which he regarded as of the strictest relevance to his own person and ministry, it is

[1] *Ibid.*, p. 59.

difficult to see exactly how or why he can or should be trusted anywhere else.'[1]

The logic of this is somewhat difficult to follow. If, for instance, an absent-minded professor tells me that the train for Penzance leaves Waterloo at noon and I find that in fact it leaves Paddington half an hour before, I do not conclude that my informant is a liar, nor that he is ill-disposed towards me, nor that his reputation as a scholar rests on a fraud. I take him for what he is, and do not suppose that being a great authority on Homer makes him a reliable substitute for a time-table. Although this is a very imperfect analogy indeed, it has at least this force: Jesus Christ came into the world to be its Saviour, not an authority on biblical criticism. I do not feel my salvation insecure because I believe that Jesus was 'mistaken' in ascribing the authorship of the second Psalm to David, or because he seemed more certain than I am able to be that the commandments were given by 'Moses'. I know him for what he is, and see no reason at all why the Saviour of the world should at the time of his incarnation have been infallible in every field of human knowledge, even the *minutiae* of Old Testament scholarship.

Moreover, Dr Packer does not examine in detail our Lord's reported use of the Old Testament. Such an examination would yield the interesting result that it appears to have been highly selective. Whether we are to conclude that some Old Testament books were more precious to him than others, that some seemed more

[1] R. V. G. Tasker, *The Old Testament in the New Testament*, p. 37.

'inspired', or simply that we are not given a complete account of our Lord's quotations from the Old Testament, we cannot tell. What we can say is that there is at least presumptive evidence that an interpretation of the matter other than Dr Packer's is possible, and we can say with equal certainty that for Dr Packer to have the right to be as dogmatic as he is would require much ampler evidence than he or anyone else has at his disposal. On a strict use of evidence we may say that Dr Packer (or anyone else) can only say what Jesus believed about *part* of the Old Testament.

We must also look at Dr Packer's treatment of verbal inspiration. He commits himself to the view that the scriptural view of Scripture is 'What Scripture says, God says'. When we hear or read Scripture, what impinges on our mind (whether we realize it or not) is the speech of God Himself.'[1] This must be so, according to this argument, since it was necessary for God to ensure that the words written were such as did in fact convey the truth of his Word: 'if the words were not wholly God's, then their teaching could not be wholly God's'. Again, 'if God gave the Scriptures for a practical purpose—to make men wise unto salvation through faith in Christ—it is a safe inference that He never permits them to become so corrupted that they no longer fulfil it'.[2] It is significant that when Dr Packer passes from the realm of dogmatic assertion to deal with actual reality he speaks of a 'safe inference', for apart from some dogmatic presupposition about the necessity of verbal inspiration, no one as well acquainted with bibli-

[1] *Op. cit.*, p. 89.   [2] *Ibid.*, p. 90.

cal scholarship as Dr Packer is could suppose for a moment that the words of Scripture are or can be demonstrated to be 'wholly God's'. If it be argued, as it is by some Conservative Evangelicals, that could we only come by the original version of Scripture we should then have a text verbally inspired and 'wholly God's', we can but say that it is hard to see how such a version of Scripture could be recognized, if ever found, and that it is curious that valuable evidence, indispensable for salvation, has been in fact so lost that we should not know it even if we saw it. The sort of certainty that Dr Packer desires has in fact been denied us.

3 *The Conservative Evangelical Position*

To turn now to more general comments on the Conservative Evangelical position as a whole, perhaps we should note first that it strains the evidence a good deal beyond what it *necessarily* substantiates. The teaching of our Lord about the witness of the Old Testament Scriptures to his work does not *necessarily* prove that in all and in every part those writings are to be taken as authoritative. Nor does the fact that he appealed to the Old Testament sayings at the time of his Temptation *necessarily* prove that he accepted in this sense the authority of the written Word. In each case the evidence does not *require* any different attitude to the authority of the Bible than is held by Roman Catholic or modern critical scholars. To take the Old Testament seriously is not the same as taking it literally.

Similarly, those who write from this point of view

do not reckon with the fact that the texts Dr Bromiley cites from the New Testament in support of his case (I Timothy 3.16; II Peter 1.21, 3.16) are capable of quite a different interpretation than he puts upon them. Quite apart from the fact that these citations are from passages which most modern scholars would regard as not genuinely apostolic, the argument can remain on grounds which Conservative Evangelicals will recognize. For it is perfectly possible to believe that men spoke from God as they were moved by the Holy Spirit, and that every Scripture inspired by God is profitable in the way described, without drawing the conclusions about the written word of Scripture which they draw. To assume that 'God-breathed', 'inspired by God', and 'moved by the Holy Spirit' mean, and can only mean, what Conservative Evangelicals believe them to mean— this is to beg the very question at issue.

But what is to be made of the claim that our Lord accepted the Pentateuch as written by Moses or Psalm 110 as composed by David (Matthew 22.41 ff.; Mark 12.28 f.; Luke 20.42)? In their comments on these passages the writers in the *New Bible Commentary* assume the Davidic authorship of the Psalm. One of them says that if the Psalm did not come from David our Lord's words could have no weight with us now, whatever weight they might have had with his hearers then.[1] Another believes that in this case so much of the argument turns on our Lord's being right about the Davidic authorship of this Psalm that 'we hold . . . that our Lord's attribution of the Psalm to David must foreclose

[1] *Op. cit.*, p. 859.

the question of the authorship of all who accept his authority'.[1]

No allowance is here made for the possibility of our Lord's consciously accepting the popular opinion of his day, or for the still greater likelihood that within the limits of his human knowledge during his incarnate life he actually believed, as did the other men of his time, that Moses was the author of the Pentateuch, and David of this Psalm, when in fact it was not so in either case. There are obviously deep theological issues into which this is not the place to enter fully; but it may be asked whether it is not on the verge of the Monophysite heresy to suppose that our Lord's human knowledge was perfect. We may remember that on matters of greater moment than the authorship of a Psalm he claimed to be in ignorance (e.g. Mark 13.32). But on the particular question of the Davidic authorship of Psalm 110, Dr Hebert is undoubtedly right in saying that there are two issues here. If it can be maintained on scholarly grounds that this authorship is likely or even probable, that is one thing. But 'we must not invoke our Lord's authority to decide a question he was not answering'.[2] In this particular saying he is answering a question about the nature and function of the Messiah, not about the authorship of the Psalm. Are not these words of James Orr, quoted by Dr Hebert, apt?

It may be readily admitted that when Jesus used popular language about 'Moses' and 'Isaiah' he did

---

[1] *Ibid.*, p. 831.
[2] A. G. Hebert, *Fundamentalism and the Church of God*, p. 69. (Published in USA as *Fundamentalism and the Church*.)

nothing more than designate certain books, and need not be understood as giving *ex cathedra* judgments on the intricate questions which the contents of these books raise. Had such questions been put to him for decision, he would probably have dealt with them as he did with the appeal about inheritance: 'Man, who made me a judge or a divider over you?'

This somewhat detailed examination of this aspect of the Bible's witness to its own authority shows that, as in other aspects of their arguments, Dr Bromiley and Dr Packer claim too much without regard to other possible interpretations of the evidence. The texts do not necessarily mean what they insist they must mean.

The general impression created by Conservative Evangelical writings on this theme is that without their characteristic emphasis on the written Word we should be left without any certainty in religion at all. For them the value of their conviction that the Bible is and claims to be an external, final standard of doctrine appears to be that, since the truth of God has been written down, man can 'know where he is': it is for him to believe what has been written down under the inspiration of God. Whether God intends men to have this kind of security, how such written truth is to be related to human knowledge as a whole, and what can be the spiritual value of insisting that Balaam's ass really spoke, we cannot now enquire; but it is not unfair to suggest that this view of biblical authority—which is much more modern than its exponents admit, since it really started as a reaction from theological liberalism—rests upon a quite materialistic understanding of the nature of knowledge. This is in its way ironical, since Conservative Evangelicals often (and not without some reason) accuse those from whom they differ of being unduly influenced by scientific ways of thought. Yet in actual fact it is they themselves who are its victims in that they insist after the fashion of a rather outmoded 'scientific' outlook on regarding only what is written down and literally true as being at all reliable: 'this is not to take the Bible as it is, but to impose upon it an alien standard derived from the materialistic thinking of our scientific age'.[1] That apart, however, the main difficulty is about the basic presupposition of this whole attitude to the Bible. Is it God's way to reveal himself in such wise as to confront men with written statements to be woven into a dogmatic pattern which they must take or leave? Does the truth as it is in Jesus win its way with men thus? Is this really in keeping, on the one hand with the ways of God as we know them in Christ, or on the other with the faithful proclamation of Christ crucified which has for so long been the finest feature of Conservative Evangelical preaching? Is the appeal to the written Word, or to the Word made flesh?

To those who hold different views about biblical authority, Conservative Evangelicals often seem to read the Bible 'in the flat'. They seem to refuse to recognize clear differences between various types of biblical material, and not to make due allowance for the manifest imperfections of the human authors of Scripture. They insist, for example, in the literal rather than the

[1] A. G. Hebert, *Fundamentalism and the Church of God*, p. 87.

parabolic interpretation of Jonah and the historical rather than the 'mythological' character of Genesis 1 and 2. This is not because they are unaware of the arguments by which other Christian scholars have been convinced; but because they are persuaded that if they once let go of their view of biblical authority their dogmatic structure would totter. They must insist on the historicity of Adam (and therefore of Genesis 1 and 2) because of the use made of Adam in Paul's argument in Romans 5.12 ff. In other words, the enquiry is not open. Dogmatic vested interests are at stake; and the Bible is invoked to support a system of doctrine derived from a particular understanding of the Bible, instead of discovering what Scripture really is and what it really teaches as the preparation for building whatever dogmatic structure Scripture really requires.[1]

This consideration of historic ways of regarding biblical authority—Roman Catholic and Calvinist, 'modern' and 'conservative'—has led us each time to the same questions. How does God's truth gain the consent of man? What does God will to happen when a man is moved to faith? How does he desire men to respond to the story of his grace? We must turn to these questions in our next chapter, for whoever answers such questions reveals in what way he understands the Gospel.

---

[1] For a very full and learned exposition of Conservative Evangelical attitudes, see the symposium *Revelation and the Bible*, ed. C. F. H. Henry.

IV

TRUTH'S VICTORY

1 The Authority Exercised by Jesus Christ

AS FAR AS Christianity is concerned revelation is given in a person, not simply in his words, but in himself; not in some aspects of himself or in certain of his works, but in his total self. It is not in his words or deeds separately or together, but in himself. Moreover, this person is declared to be the culmination of a series of divine acts whereby God accomplishes the redemption of a fallen world. This is the meaning that lies within the phrase 'the living God'; and since the Bible takes much more seriously than men ever dare to the truth that actions speak louder than words, it declares that God's self-disclosure takes place through these mighty deeds and in this person in whom they reach their finality and victory.

If this is so, we should look at Jesus Christ if we wish to discover the nature of authority and the way in which it is exercised, for on this reckoning he is not only the crux of revelation but also and for that very reason the place at which to understand this mystery: 'All authority in heaven and on earth has been given to me' (Matthew 28.18). The significant thing appears to be not so much the way in which Jesus spoke with authority, nor the magisterial way in which he claims to be a greater than Moses although we must note the fact that the one who could replace 'Thus saith the Lord' with 'I say unto you' is evidently conscious of exercising authority—but rather his general claim to be doing the works of God, to have inaugurated the age to come, to be the means whereby the reign of God is at work in the world in a new and especially significant way. Herrmann remarked that Jesus seemed to know no more sacred duty than to point men to himself. The Word was made flesh and dwelt among us; God's glory is to be seen in the face of Jesus Christ. As a result of this ministry, men were confronted with the very activity of God himself, with the self-disclosure of God. It is of the utmost importance to discover, if we may, how this revelation was brought home to men.

The evidence suggests that our Lord rejected most of the ways in which popular acclaim is won. He did not promulgate a doctrinal system which was to be accepted by his disciples; he steadfastly refused to gain the open-mouthed applause of men by providing signs from heaven; he demanded that men should think for themselves rather than accept second-hand convictions. There were no doubt many ways in which the religious teacher of his day could win a considerable following; and we may suppose that there were many, then as now, who were ready to be told what to believe and what to do. Yet throughout his ministry Jesus sought no other assent than that which was spontaneously given by those who for themselves recognized who he was and what he was doing. It was the insight and trust of those who could see the signs of the times and were

prepared to commit themselves to the Lord's anointed
that he counted precious.

Let us recall some evidence. The question to the
disciples at Caesarea Phillipi seeks to discover whether
the revelation he had brought had been made to those
who had been with him most, whether life with him
had evoked insight. These men had been with him: had
they understood? There was no other argument he
could bring to bear, only himself, his words and his
deeds (Mark 8.27 ff.). The disciples of John the Baptist
are told that there is no other answer to the question
'Art thou he that should come, or do we look for
another?' (AV) than the evidence supplied and what he
had been proclaiming to the multitudes. They must
make up their own minds whether the message was true
and whether such works were indeed the signs that the
Kingdom had come (Matthew 11.1-6). The parables of
Jesus are designed to confront his hearers with an issue
about which they must make a decision; and the fact
that men can so easily see the truth and turn away from
it with scornful hatred is most tragically to be seen in
the terrible words which ascribe to the devil the works
of God (Matthew 12.22 ff.). It is, moreover, one of the
works of the Holy Spirit to quicken insight (John 14.16,
26; 15.26); and it is clear that Jesus thought it better to
wait until men had been brought to see things for themselves than to indoctrinate them with truths which they
could only know on his authority and not in the deep
places of their own souls. Only when men sincerely live
by what they have learned for themselves can they
grow in the knowledge of God; and those who do not

honestly live by what they allege to have accepted cannot learn more until they have begun to be honest with what truth they have seen (Luke 16.31).

Our Lord's work as a teacher must be to disclose reality and seek to persuade men to be honest about it, to recognize it for what it is, to commit themselves to it with mind and soul and strength. Part of the meaning of the Temptations of Jesus is surely that in that experience he wrestled with the problem how to win men's assent to his mission; and the victory over Satan is the rejection of the wrong sort of authority and the setting aside of unworthy ways of winning popular support. It seems as if he saw then what he certainly feared throughout his ministry, that men would come to believe in him for wrong reasons; and few things are more striking about our Lord's ministry than his constant refusal to bludgeon men into belief, and his incredibly calm acceptance of the fact of their unbelief. 'He could do no mighty work there . . . because of their unbelief' (Mark 6.5; cf. Matthew 14.58). The restraint of it—when he could at one stroke have shown them who he was! The prophet who looks for insight and trust from his hearers must have the infinite patience to watch them turn from him in unbelief and to wait until his message has carried its own weight in their minds. He must reject the way of peddling ready-made convictions so dear at all times to the fanatic's closed mind. He must understand that truth is too sacred to be tested by mass-appeals and Gallup polls. A person is a person, whose consent must be free and responsible if it is to be significant at all. Better to wait for truth's

long delayed victory than to compromise one moment
with the propagandist's meretricious speed.

It needs to be clearly recognized that the basis of our
Lord's appeal was himself. 'Follow me,' 'come unto me'
and 'ye will not come unto me' indicate sufficiently that
what he offered to men was himself. He seeks to win
men's acceptance of the truth that had come in him
(John 1.14, 18.37). His words and deeds served to indicate what manner of man he was and what kind of
work he had come to do; and all the time it is a person
addressing persons, seeking to gain their recognition of
and their self-commitment to himself. He sought to
exercise no authority over men that was not personal,
both in the way in which it was exercised, and in the
way in which it was recognized and accepted.

2   *Forsyth and Temple on Authority*

John Owen wrote in the seventeenth century :

Light manifests its selfe. Whatever is Light doth
so : that is, it doth whatever is necessary on its own
part for its manifestation and discovery. . . . Light
requires neither proofe nor Testimony for its
Evidence. Let the Sun arise in the firmament, and
there is no need of Witnesses to prove and confirme
unto a seeing man that it is day. A small candle will
so do. Let the least child bring a candle into a roome
that before was darke, and it would be madnesse to
go about to prove by substantiall Witnesses, men of
gravity and authority, that Light is brought in. Doth
it not evince itsselfe, with an Assurance above all that
can be obteined by any Testimony whatever ? What-

ever is Light, either naturally or morally so, is revealed by its being so.[1]

Sympathetic with this approach is a modern discussion, once described by an Anglican theologian as 'one of the greatest treatments of the subject of authority in the English, if not in any, language, P. T. Forsyth's book, *The Principle of Authority*'.[2] Forsyth[3] argues that the truth of our redemption in Christ 'becomes its own authority. . . . A redeeming Christ thus becomes his own authority with us.'

> We can only believe in redemption to any practical purpose by believing in the Redeemer—by a personal relation of committal for ever to that Person and His act of capture. . . . We can have no standard for our absolute Judge and Saviour. We know him with at least as much certainty as we know any fact or law, cosmic or psychic; by another order of knowledge perhaps, but with far more intimacy. . . .[4]

---

[1] John Owen, *Of the Divine Originall, Authority, Self-evidencing Light, and Power of the Scriptures* (Oxford, 1658-9), pp. 72-3.

[2] R. R. Williams, *Authority in the Apostolic Age*, p. 119.

[3] P. T. Forsyth (1848-1921), Principal of Hackney College, London (1901-21), is often reckoned the greatest and most original theologian in Congregationalism in recent times. He protested in his day against a good deal of theological liberalism, especially as propounded by R. J. Campbell, then Minister of the City Temple, London. Forsyth believed that an undogmatic Christianity was a contradiction in terms. He anticipated the 'realism of much modern theology without the extravagances of Barthianism'. An excellent memoir of him is included in the 1938 edition of his *The Work of Christ*.

[4] P. T. Forsyth, *The Principle of Authority*, pp. 20-21.

As Forsyth expounded this view, he distinguished three elements in authority.

(1) However much we may in the first part of our religious discipline depend on some sort of external authority, such as statements about religion made by those who are in positions of religious authority over us, the soul cannot live and grow on such an external authority. It is only when the object of religion itself becomes an authority for the person, for the soul, that we pass from our minority and achieve adult status.[1]

(2) When we have come to religious maturity, 'our only authority must be faith's object itself in some direct self-revelation of it. Our authority is what takes the initiative with our faith. . . . Our only final religious authority is the creative object of our religion, to whom we owe ourselves. Every statement about God is challengeable till God states Himself, in His own way, by His own Son, His own Spirit, His own Word, His own Church, to our soul, which he remakes in the process.'[2]

(3) Forsyth argues that 'the only religious authority must be some action of God's creative self-revelation, and not simply an outside witness to it'. A subsequent phrase indicates how he understands this. 'Christ's real presence with us in the Holy Ghost as our active Saviour.[3]

It is in the light of these three interweaving convictions that we are to understand Forsyth's subsequent exclamation:

[1] *Ibid.*, pp. 21-22.   [2] *Ibid.*, p. 22.   [3] *Ibid.*, p. 23.

Who shall tell me what to believe about Christ? None can. No Church can. No book can; no saint, no theologian. None but Christ himself in actual presence—it may be without a word that I could report, or a theme I could frame—by overwhelming my soul with its greatness and its evil, its joy and its salvation, in his invincible word of death, resurrection and glory.[1]

This must not be thought to imply that Forsyth thought that the testimony of the Bible and of the Church was irrelevant or superfluous. There is ample evidence that he prized objective standards of faith far more deeply than most of his contemporaries, against whom he was often in vigorous controversy. He will have nothing to do with a religion that is a mere spirituality; and he speaks with due reverence of the way in which the Scriptures, the Church and the Sacraments anchor our thought to the historical character of our religion and deliver us from mere opinions. Yet the principal value of such testimony, which may be marred here and there by some defect in a historical document or some moral flaw in a preacher, is that they are made revelation by God who reveals himself through them. All human testimonies may 'fade into the rear when they have done their work. . . . So long as they have brought us to direct communion with God, with Christ . . . and stirred the evidence of his Spirit's action and power in our soul's new life.'[2]

When they have done their proper work, when they have introduced us personally to God and left

[1] *Ibid.*, p. 70.   [2] *Ibid.*, p. 23.

us together, it is not fatal if we find flaws in their logic, character, or faith. . . . Defects in Church, Bible, or apostle, defects in the logic of creed . . . need not destroy the real religious witness they bear on the whole, their sacramental mediation of the Gospel to us. Secure in the God to whom they have led us, we turn at our ease and leisure to examine their flaws with a quiet and kindly mind, knowing that they do not cost us our soul's life.[1]

Indeed, Forsyth welcomed the critical study of the Bible, because he took it as 'meant to disengage crude religion from all temporary and pedagogic authority, however valuable, and to force us for our moral manhood upon the only authority truly religious'.[2]

The real question is, 'Can the Jesus of yesterday be everyone's most present Christ today and for ever?' To handle that question successfully, says Forsyth, we must get rid of the notion of saving truths in the sense of truths that save ('that is mere Orthodoxy').

> Truths about Christ are really sure to the Church only as they arise out of its experience of Christ. . . . Truths about salvation rise out of experience of salvation. . . . We shall be sure of an actual, final authority in proportion as we have had the experience of being absolutely mastered by the moral act of redemption which made Christ King of human history. . . . Our authority . . . is Jesus Christ, our Redeemer.[3]

It is interesting to compare this with Archbishop William Temple's teaching:[4]

[1] *Ibid.,* p. 24.   [2] *Ibid.,* p. 22.   [3] *Ibid.,* pp. 71-2.
[4] William Temple, *Nature, Man, and God,* pp. 321, 322.

Knowledge of God can be fully given only in a person, never in a doctrine, still less in a formless faith, whatever that might be. . . . The life of faith is not the acceptance of doctrine any more than the life of the natural man is the acceptance of mathematical equations, or the life of the artist is the acceptance of artistic canons. The canons and equations assist the effective adjustment and intercourse of organism and environment, but the life of art, or of mere organic continuance, has its being in that adjustment and intercourse. . . . Faith is not the holding of correct doctrines, but personal fellowship with the living God. Correct doctrine will express this, assist it, and issue from it; incorrect doctrine will misrepresent this and hinder or prevent it. Doctrine is of an importance too great to be exaggerated; but its place is secondary, not primary. I do not believe in any creed, but I use certain creeds to express, to conserve, and to deepen my belief in God. What is offered to man's apprehension in any specific revelation is not truth concerning God, but the living God himself.

Such a line of argument seems to be in line with the idea or authority to be deduced from the New Testament, and particularly from the teaching and ministry of Jesus Christ. What is disclosed is disclosed through a person; and it is left to carry its own weight with those to whom the revelation is made. There is an appeal to insight. Another modern theologian has written: 'God is not "authoritarian" in the exercise of his authority, for authoritarianism is but the *ersatz* robe assumed by tyrants and dictators who possess no real authority.'[1]

[1] Alan Richardson, *Christian Apologetics*, p. 222.

3 *The Place of Experience*

It will be objected by some that this view of the
nature of authority and the way in which it is exercised is vague and ill-defined. It will be said that it provides no guarantees that the work of revelation will
succeed, that men will bow before the august majesty
of God's self-disclosure. Those who rightly stress the
objective element in revelation and emphasize the
givenness of the content of the Christian Faith will complain that too much is allowed for subjectivity and all
that is involved in man's appropriation of what is given
in revelation. Insofar as such protests are reminders
warning us against the empty vagaries of 'mere
spirituality', they are to be welcomed and taken most
seriously. It is, however, not out of place to ask that
such words as 'subjective' and 'experience' be freed
from prejudice and not used merely as terms of abuse.
The fact that undue emphasis on religious experience
can throw our entire apprehension of Christian truth
out of perspective, and indeed so concentrate our
thought on what we have known and felt as to leave
little or no room for more universal and objective
elements in our religion, provides us with no reason for
denying any place at all to the subjective in the life of
faith. Schleiermacher and Ritschl, with their emphasis
on experience, may inevitably, and to some extent
deservedly, have gone out of theological fashion. The
enthusiasm of the sects may properly appear effer-
vescent alongside the 'massive objectivity of the Word
of God'. But if what is revealed is to be apprehended at

all, there must be an act of insight and acceptance which, if it be at all true, cannot be devoid of rapture; and since, as we may believe, it is not God's way to disclose himself in such wise as to be apprehended after the same manner as a scientific proof or a series of dogmas, but rather to disclose himself as person to person—waiting until what he is and what he does is recognized, accepted and trusted by those to whom it is given—we cannot expect that the subjective element in religion will be minimized in a true understanding of the Christian revelation. And if it appears that such an understanding of Christian truth and the way in which it is brought home to men leaves the issue much less precise and well-defined than do other views of authority where recourse is had to infallibilities and impregnable rocks, the answer must be that this is necessarily so. It is God's purpose to bring us into the glorious liberty of his children, and that the pathway to that land of deliverance is walked in faith and not by sight. To trust finally in any external guarantee of faith is to fall away from faith altogether, and to demand sight. As Berdyaev wrote:

Faith knows nothing of external guarantees, that is, of course, faith as an original experience of the life of the Spirit. It is only in the secondary exoteric sphere of the religious life that we find guarantees and a general attempt to compel faith. To demand guarantees and proofs of faith is to fail to understand its very nature by denying the free heroic act which it inspires. In really authentic and original religious experience, to the existence of which the history of the human spirit bears abundant witness, faith

springs up without the aid of guarantees and compelling proofs, without any external coercion or the
use of authority.[1]

Berdyaev sets the issue sharply; not too sharply, for
we are concerned with no mere clash between two
opposing schools of theology. The question is what sort
of God it is in whom we believe? What is the response
which his disclosure of himself is destined to evoke? If
it is believed that faith should be equated with *the
acceptance of truths*, whether as formulated by Nicaea
or Chalcedon, whether they bear the imprimatur of the
Vatican or Geneva, whether it be a party-line from
Catholic or Evangelical, we shall expect clear-cut doctrines, neat definitions and precise exclusions. But if
we believe that faith is to be understood as *personal
commitment* to One who reveals himself to us in grace,
whose purpose is less to produce orthodox believers
than to train loving children, who is patient with honest
fumblings after truth, whose Son was so critical of the
precise and authoritarian religion of the scribes and
Pharisees that they could not suffer him, than we need
not be over-anxious if men's apprehension of him
cannot always be neatly comprehended within schemes
of doctrine or even within inspired writings. Our understanding of his way with us is as impossible to describe
properly as our relationships with those we love,
though we are blessedly certain of the sublime reality
of both. When we have striven to our best ability to
mark out and reckon on his ways, we are driven to confess that we see through a glass darkly.

[1] N. Berdyaev, *Freedom and the Spirit*, p. 105.

If we are right in believing that it is God's purpose in redemption to gain personal trust in his grace and to train loving children in the ways of freedom and responsibility, then we must agree with Forsyth: to insist on 'the need of an authority without, not to agree with the authority within, but to dominate it' must reveal a lack of faith in the possibility of human freedom and in the ways which God has chosen to create and nourish it. We are impelled to ask with John Oman whether, if submission to truth be the object in view, the end would not have been better served 'had God absolutely subjected men to himself from the beginning'. Indeed, we may go further with John Oman:

> If the obedience of mere submission will satisfy the heart of God, then we can only say that the method God has employed with man is chiefly distinguished from the method he has employed with the planets by the chaos it has permitted. Were it only desired that man should differ from the planets in being conscious of the law he obeyed, why, instead of a slow revelation presenting ideals for an imperfect striving, was not unconditional obedience effected from the very beginning by a proclamation of God's mind and will which none might deny and none disobey? . . . If God can be satisfied with mere subordination, if his purpose is not to set man free, in the conscious discovery of his own place and willing acceptance of it, in the final harmony of God's purpose within him and God's purpose without him, this strange perplexing struggle for existence, this world of imperfect endeavour and plenteous failure, is merely a proof of his incompetence. . . . The truly marvellous thing in God's revelation of himself is not that it subdues man to his

obedience, which were easy, but that it makes men free with the liberty of God's children, which is a difficulty only omnipotence could overcome.[1]

Because of what God has disclosed of his own nature and being, because of what we may deduce about his ways with men, an exact description of the way in which he exercises authority over them cannot be provided. What may be insisted upon is that this authority is personal and is exercised with full respect for the personality of those to whom the revelation of truth is made. What is deduced from this must inevitably be marked with that lack of detailed precision which is characteristic of all truly personal relationships.

4   Truths of Revelation

But, it may be asked, what of the 'truths of revelation'? What about propositions about God and about what he has done for mankind in Jesus Christ?

In a well-known book Dr A. M. Farrer, now Warden of Keble College, Oxford, criticizes with great vigour the kind of thinking so far expounded—although he takes his illustration from the Jewish philosopher Martin Buber, rather than from Forsyth or Oman. Since he clearly fears that to emphasize the 'personalism' of the Christian religion may lead to a denigration of rational theology, it will be well to look closely at his argument.

An autobiographical passage near the beginning of

[1] John Oman, *Vision and Authority*, 8th ed., p. 95, 97.

The Glass of Vision[1] records that Dr Farrer was brought
up in a personalism 'which might satisfy the most
ardent of Dr Buber's disciples. I thought of myself as
set over against deity as one man faces another across
a table, except that God was invisible and indefinitely
great. And I hoped that he would signify his presence
to me by colloquy; but neither out of the Scripture I
read nor in the prayers I tried to make did any mental
voice answer me. . . . Nothing came: no "other" stood
beside me, no shadow of presence fell upon me.' His
deliverance from this frustration came, we are told,
through reading Spinoza's *Ethics*, from which he
learned not to set God before his face but to attempt
to see him as the underlying cause of his thinking,
especially of those thoughts in which he tried to think
of him. 'And this is why, when Germans set their eye-
balls and pronounce the terrific words "He speaks to
thee" I am sure, indeed, that they are saying something,
but I am still more sure that they are not speaking to
my condition.'

This surprisingly unashamed argument from one
type of religious experience can hardly be taken to
prove more than Dr Farrer's inability to verify from
experience the truth of Dr Buber's teaching. The relevance of this piece of autobiography for our immediate
purpose, however, is that this early experience gave
rise in Dr Farrer's mind to a deep suspicion of anything
like the personalism in which he was reared, principally
on the ground that it seemed to him to lead to a denigration of rational theology. This would, indeed, be a

[1] *Ibid.*, p. 8.

fatal defect; and if it could be proved to be necessarily
the case that a personalist understanding of the Christian religion led to a neglect of rational theology those
who accept it would have seriously to rethink the
whole basis of their theology. It may be recognized
without hesitation that some forms of personalist thinking fall into this error. But the question is whether a personalist theology is *true*, and whether it *necessarily*
leads its adherents to estimate too lightly the value of
rational theology.

It may be claimed that those who emphasize the personal character of God's dealings with his children do
not isolate rational theology in such a way as to give
the intellectual aspect of religion a disproportionate
value. Yet personalist theology by no means sets aside
rational reflection upon the meaning of God's self disclosure which is apprehended by faith. If it does not
exalt the truths of revelation to a place of primary importance, as if they were the elementary stuff of religion, it does recognize that they have very considerable authority indeed—provided that they are properly
and necessarily derived from revelation itself.

Dr John Baillie has well described the relation between revelation and propositions about revelation. He
takes up a point made by Dr C. H. Dodd in his commentary on *Romans*, that 'for Paul faith is that attitude
in which . . . we rely utterly on the sufficiency of God';
it does not mean 'belief in a proposition, though doubt-
less intellectual beliefs are involved when we come to
think it out'. Dr Baillie goes on to use an analogy from
human friendship:

When I trust somebody, or have *fiducia* in him, I am manifestly at the same time believing certain things about him to be true, yet I may find it very difficult to say exactly what those things are—I may even flounder in the attempt to assign the reasons for my trust. This is why the formal develop-ment of dogma, and especially of Christological dogma, hardly got under way until the Christian mission had been confronted with the scepticism of the Greek mind.[1]

With this may be compared the well-known words of William Temple, who likened theologians to musical critics, analysing and summarizing. His emphatic con-clusion was that

there is no such thing as revealed truth. There are truths of revelation, that is to say, propositions which express the result of correct thinking concerning revelation; but they are not themselves directly re-vealed. On the other hand, this does not involve the result that there need be anything vague or indefinite about revelation itself.[2]

To insist on this distinction between revelation and truths of revelation, and to insist on the personal char-acter of the act in which revelation is given and re-ceived, does not necessarily deny or minimize the im-portance of 'the result of correct thinking concerning revelation'.

There is, however, another point to be taken up from Dr Farrer's outburst; and it concerns his emphasis on

[1] John Baillie, *The Idea of Revelation in Recent Thought*, p. 92.
[2] *Nature, Man, and God*, p. 317.

'reason'. Indeed, this emphasis and his predilection for Aristotle raise the large question whether he has not fallen into the error, brought about in Christian theology by an uncritical acceptance of Greek ways of thought, of thinking that there is a particular 'faculty', in this case, reason, in view of which man may be regarded as human. To raise the issue is to risk the charge of being party to that belittling of reason which is so disastrous a feature of much modern theology, and a good deal of modern philosophy as well. But the question must be asked whether Emil Brunner's attack on this way of thinking is not justified.[1] He suggests that we must reject any notion that the only thing about man which matters is the divine reason dwelling in him, which means that 'it is . . . an abstract, impersonal, general principle . . . which makes men human'; and he argues that we should realize that 'the Christian concept of personality . . . is the call of God, summoning me, this individual man, to communion with him'. *This* is what makes a man a person. We ought not to suppose that Christ and his Gospel are addressed to the reason alone, but to the whole personality. To use Dr Brunner's words again, 'a divine *I* calls me *Thou* and attests to me that I, this individual man, being here and being so, am seen and called by God from all eternity'.

The Gospel in all its gift and demand, therefore, comes to us not simply in the form 'Will you accept this as true?', for that is but part of what happens. The real question is, 'What think ye of Christ?' It is a question of total commitment to or total rejection of Christ.

[1] *Christianity and Civilization*, vol. i, p. 94.

To treat reason as if it were the measure of all things is nothing more than a misunderstanding and a perversion of that utterly and intimately personal relationship in which every man stands to the source of all authority.

5   *How Faith Comes*

But, it may be asked, how are those to whom God reveals himself enabled to perceive what he discloses? How is faith kindled, and how is insight awakened?

It is perhaps not quite fair to say that those whose characteristic emphasis is on the rational nature of Christian truth sometimes give the impression that faith is to be reached at the end of a series of rational arguments, and that the task of evangelism is to provide such arguments in a convincing fashion. To challenge any such assumption is by no means to deny the need for disciplined thought.

Rather is it to draw attention to two facts which are frequently overlooked when Christianity is presented as a number of truths which, once understood, are likely to be accepted. It is surely a plain verdict of Christian experience that very few people indeed are brought to faith in this way. To hear and understand a lucid explanation of what the Christian faith is, and what it is not, will clear the mind of many a misunderstanding; it will prepare the way for 'Lord, I believe; help thou mine unbelief'. But this of itself will not create that experience in which insight comes and faith is declared.

In a famous passage near the beginning of I Corin-

D

thians, St Paul uses words which may be taken as typical
of the Gospel : the natural man is incapable of discern-
ing spiritual things. There is no need to emphasize the
rhetorical passages in which he quotes the Old Testament's words about God catching the wise in their own
craftiness and knowing the thoughts of the wise that
they are futile. But it is striking that he recognizes the
focus of revelation in Christ crucified (1.23), and declares that in Christ was displayed a wisdom besides
which the world's wisdom is shown up for folly. St Paul
goes on to affirm that truth of this sort, so baffling to
the man of this world that he engineers the crucifixion,
can only be discerned by the spiritual man. 'The unspiritual man does not receive the gifts of the Spirit of
God; for they are folly to him, and he is not able to
understand them, because they are spiritually discerned'
(2.14). To be given this discernment, however, is to share
the mind of Christ. The whole passage together with its
context strongly argues for the fact of a spiritual blindness which makes it impossible for God's self-disclosure
to be understood and accepted save as he himself gives
sight and understanding. This disability of the natural
man is not due simply to wrong-thinking. It is not as if
the unspiritual man could not count or was faulty in
logic. The root of the malaise lies much deeper. Man
cannot see God's truth for what it is because he is in a
state of sinful rebellion : he has 'collided with the moral
unity of things, with the absolute holiness of God'.[1] Insight requires moral as well as intellectual integrity;
not for nothing is it written that the pure in heart shall

[1] P. T. Forsyth, *op. cit.*, p. 45.

see God. St Paul 'saw' on the road to Damascus.[1]

But, if we are to believe what is taught us in the New Testament, moral integrity is a quality which men cannot acquire for themselves, even though in search of it they endure great spiritual discipline. So we are confronted with an impasse: without moral as well as intellectual integrity man cannot truly perceive God's self-disclosure and cannot therefore apprehend revelation; yet he cannot raise himself to the level of moral integrity. It is when we face this dilemma that we are able to understand another fundamental part of the witness of the New Testament, that only God himself can reveal to us our plight and enable us to see him as he reveals himself as to be moved to faith. It is the work of the Holy Spirit to awaken insight; and in the last resort the real answer to the question 'what happens when a man hears the truth of the Gospel and accepts it?' is that faith has been kindled by the Holy Spirit. No man can say 'Jesus is Lord' without the Spirit (I Corinthians 12.3).

It is said to be the fault of some Christians to desire to contain the Holy Spirit within official channels, just as it could be said that other sorts of Christians are never more sure of his presence with them than when they flout any and every ecclesiastical law and reject almost any theological truth! Perhaps these misunderstandings of the Holy Spirit's operations have contributed in no small degree to that neglect of them in

---

[1] G. B. Caird, *Principalities and Powers*, p. 85, observes: 'Only by such an experience, which healed the blindness of his inner eye, could the historic fact become visible to him.'

theology which is frequently and properly deplored. Nevertheless, any group of Christians which does not make due reckoning with 'no one "can say Jesus is Lord" except by the Holy Spirit must be judged to have missed the depth of the New Testament's understanding of the nature of authority and the way in which it is exercised. The right question to ask about Christian certainty is not 'How do I reach it?' but 'How does it reach me?' Essential Christian certainty is 'not a rational but a miraculous thing'.[1]

This argument is naturally an offence to those who will go no further than strict logic can take them, though it may mitigate the offence if it be at once admitted that the argument is not intended to imply in the very least that what are often called Christian evidences are of no value. The so-called 'proofs' for the existence of God, for example, can hardly be held to prove in the strict sense that God exists, though they may be thought to indicate some probability that belief in God is not nonsense. In this way they may help to shake the unbeliever's confidence that he alone is talking sense, or confirm the believer in his faith when he suffers the assaults of doubt and fears that his faith is built on the sands of wishful thinking. Similarly, the arguments which provide proof of the historical worth of the Gospels serve to strengthen our faith that in believing in Jesus Christ we are not paying homage to an imaginary being who never had any actual existence: that he lived, and died 'under Pontius Pilate', anchors him in history. Yet to prove that a prophetic

[1] P. T. Forsyth, *op. cit.*, pp. 18, 52.

teacher actually lived and worked in Galilee and Jerusalem at a specific period in the world's history does
not, and cannot, of itself convince any of the truth
about him which Christians have been led to believe
and proclaim, any more than to put the utmost possible
weight on the 'proofs' for God's existence can convince
a man of the reality of God. The meaning of the Exodus
and of the Passion of Christ is not made evident by
historical proof. Nor is the case carried to its conclusion
by a careful and compelling exposition of what meaning these and other significant events have been held to
bear by generations of Jews and Christians. Unless there
be the awakening of insight, unless the person who
studies these proofs and hears these expositions comes
to the point of seeing for himself that what is proclaimed is true, the whole weight of religious testimony
has so far failed in his case.

The phrase 'generations of Jews and Christians' suggests a line of argument to which is sometimes attached
the very greatest importance. Beyond the expositions
provided by reason is there not the deliverance of the
Church? Whatever view of the Church may be taken,
it is the belief of all Christians that the Church has the
task of handing on from generation to generation the
faith 'once for all delivered to the saints' through the
transmission and exposition of the Bible, the symbols
and confessions of faith, and worship in one or other
of the traditions of Christendom. From one point of
view it is difficult indeed to exaggerate the importance
of the service the Church renders its Lord in these ways;
yet it may be thought that its importance is exaggerated

when it is said that a man should believe because the Church declares the faith. Surely the response which the Church must seek as it proclaims the Gospel entrusted to its keeping is that those who hear it should be moved to say, 'Lord, I believe; help thou mine unbelief!' John 4.42 puts it thus: 'It is no longer because of your words that we believe, for we have heard for ourselves, and we know that this is indeed the Saviour of the world.' It is true, of course, that the faith thus evoked in Jesus Christ by the operation of the Holy Spirit is something the implications and consequences of which will only become clear through instruction and development within the fellowship of the Church. But, without such faith, a full understanding of the whole system of Christian dogma falls short of that personal response which we must needs believe the Father seeks from all his children, a response which results from an experience of illumination and purification.

Some may complain that too much has been allowed to the 'subjective' and too little to the 'objective' elements in the whole process of revelation and belief. But all discussion of the process must take full account not only of what is given but of those to whom it is given; both the objective and subjective elements are important. And it may well be that we cannot understand revelation and faith unless we learn how to hold both in a proper balance. Nor should it be forgotten that, since revelation is addressed to persons, it is inevitable that the purpose of revelation cannot be fulfilled until a personal response is made to it. In its measure, this response to what is given is as important as what is given.

In his last Gifford Lecture, Dr Leonard Hodgson reviews and sums up the main purport of the whole series:

> I have been trying to put before you what I have come to believe as a result of a life spent in the inter-permeating study of theology and philosophy. The argument of these twenty lectures is a kind of map of the course my mind has travelled through forty-seven years. It has often been concerned with questions which are not patient of demonstrative proof, where in each case all that can be done is to state as clearly as possible how one has come to see it, asking 'Cannot you see it too?'[1]

Dr Hodgson distinguishes two modes of God's self-revelation: what comes to us by a study of the universe in general, and what is given to us in his redemptive activity the record of which is to be found in the Bible. He argues that in both God's methods are the same: 'He reveals himself by doing things and inspiring men to grasp the significance of what he has done.'[2] Earlier in his lectures, Dr Hodgson has argued that 'in medicine and in mathematics, and in the arts as well as in the sciences, advances in knowledge come through men gifted with a *flair* for seeing what others do not see. These open the door through which others may pass and have their eyes opened to see it, too. Their vision is accepted as genuine insight into objective truth by those who say: "Yes, now that you have opened my eyes to it, I can see that it is so." He goes on to claim that 'the Old Testament prophets and our Lord's dis-

[1] *For Faith and Freedom*, vol. ii, p. 204.
[2] *Ibid.*, vol. ii, pp. 104 ff.

ciples were men gifted with the *flair* for seeing in the
events of Israel's history and in the Son of Mary what
other men did not. Their vision approves itself as
genuine insight, what they have seen is accepted as
objective truth, by those who in reading what they
have written have had their eyes opened to what they
saw.'[1]

The two features of the discussion which are immediately revelant to our present purpose are that (1) it contains a clear emphasis on the objectivity of revelation,
and (2) it insists that what is revealed is grasped by
those who, hearing the testimony of those who already
believe, are themselves led to believe by the same Spirit
who had earlier awakened insight and faith in those
who bore witness to what they had come to see. In such
ways, we may suppose, God reveals himself and brings
home to men what he reveals; and it appears that, since
he has made us persons with a real life of our own and
a genuine freedom to order our lives and learn to distinguish between what is false and what is true, he so
honours his image in us, and so respects the freedom he
has himself imparted, that he waits until we see for ourselves the grace and truth he has disclosed.

[1] *Ibid.*, vol. i, p. 100.

V

HOW IMPORTANT IS THE BIBLE?

THE ARGUMENT THUS far raises at least two questions which must now be faced as the book reaches its conclusion. Does the individual Christian approach the Bible alone? Again, it may well be asked, what exactly is the value and meaning of the written Scripture?

1 The Church and Scripture

If such emphasis is laid on an individual's own appropriation of Christian truth from Scripture, does it follow that he can read the Bible alone and never be bothered with what other Christians have ever thought and believed and what they think and believe today?

Such a question has only to be asked for it to be perfectly clear that the answer is No. No Christian can live in isolation from his brethren: indeed, his very act of reading the Bible relates him at once not only to those who were the human authors of Scripture but also to those through whose labours the Bible has reached him in the language wherein he was born. Moreover, the results of most attempts to read the Bible in solitude are sufficiently depressing to put commentaries at a premium! Indeed, it is to be remembered that those who take the Bible more or less literally, and interpret it out of harmony with the general sense of Christian belief, are not remarkably unanimous in their declarations of what the Bible means. It is not the 'modern' biblical scholar alone whose researches into the Scriptures do not provide 'assured' results!

Quite apart, however, from the fact that a solitary Christian is more or less a contradiction in terms and that the man who seeks to understand the Bible by himself is guilty of either ignorance or pride (or both), the plain facts are that he has a Bible at all because the Church gave it him; and without the Church he can only very partially understand it at all. The Bible is the Church's gift to him not only in the sense that it preserved the Scriptures, but also because under the guidance of the Holy Spirit, as we may believe, it chose to retain the canonical Scriptures of Israel as its Old Testament and decided which of all the variety of early Christian writings should be set within the canon and recognized as sacred. 'It did so quite naturally,' writes Dr Dodd, 'because the impulse to select was no different from the impulse that had originally led in various ways to the composition of the works. In the language of the New Testament itself, it was "to bear witness" to certain central realities that the New Testament writings were first composed, and subsequently compiled into a canon of Scripture.'[1]

The fact that in this sense the Church brought forth the Bible must not be understood as giving the Church any supremacy over Scripture. It did not create the Word of God; but it was called into being by that Word, and recognized it when confronted with it. It is not to

[1] C. H. Dodd, *The Bible Today*, p. 7.

be thought that the Scriptures became sacred because they were chosen; they were chosen because they were recognized as sacred. The Church did not confer their worth upon them: their inherent worth evoked the choice.

Moreover, it was entirely natural that the Scriptures should evolve from within the Church, for they are to a large extent the story of the creation of the people of God: this is the principal consequence of the redeeming activity of God to which the Scriptures bear witness. It is also in the highest degree natural that the Scriptures should be understood within the Church. The community which is created by God's grace understands the story of his dealings with men and holds within its corporate experience the clue to its meaning. It knows quite well that other meanings could be put upon the story in which it sees the redeeming work of God; but it claims that its interpretation is the true one. If, for instance, one could imagine Pontius Pilate thinking the crucifixion of Jesus of sufficient importance to warrant a report to Rome, the facts which he would record in his account of Good Friday might well be accurately reported. The details might call for no correction at all; and yet, in so far as he would interpret that day's work as a bothersome detail in a busy administrator's life, a mere compromise to meet the noisy wishes of a proud and disagreeable people, the Christian preacher would have to say that Pontius Pilate had not really seen the meaning of the crucifixion. There would be agreement between the two accounts, let us say, as to the fact of the crucifixion of Jesus of Nazareth; but what interpre-

tation was to be put upon the 'raw fact' would leave
room for argument. The Church would declare that in
this whose event the glory of God had been disclosed
and his grace had wrought a mighty salvation for mankind.

It is in this sort of sense that it may be truly claimed
that the Church has not only preserved the story of
Christ's work, but is also the context from within which
that story is to be truly understood. This does not mean
that the Church has never failed at any point to fulfil
its task of witness and exposition. But the Church has
always had the Scriptures to be the yardstick whereby
the truth or error of its proclamation could be judged,
and always within itself there were raised up prophets
and reformers to testify against proud or faint-hearted
dilution or distortion of the truth of God's Word. Nor
may the Church impose some tradition of its own upon
the fundamental core of witness which is its legacy
from the apostles' times. Its proper business is to
understand, interpret and proclaim the Word of God in
Scripture as the Spirit gives light upon that word. Indeed, since the New Testament (rather than the episco-
pate!) is the successor to the apostles, one of the ways
in which the Church may measure its apostolicity is to
compare its worship, teaching and action with the
Gospel as proclaimed in the New Testament.

The Church bears witness to the true meaning of the
Scriptures chiefly in two ways. These are so closely
bound together that they are separable only for purposes of discussion. They are worship (including preaching) and common life in the Body of Christ.

2 Worship and Preaching

Christian acts of worship are different in outward form as between one communion and another, and yet are essentially similar in basic structure and meaning Worship for Christians is to a very large extent a recollection, re-enactment and participation in those events to which the biblical narratives bear witness. If the worshipper sought to be no more than an intelligent spectator, he could not escape some instruction in what the Christian faith is; but the true worshipper will know that he can never be such a mere observer. He must participate and become involved. He will understand that Christian worship is a dialogue between God and his people, a family conversation in which God discloses himself through the reading of Scripture and the preaching of the Word, in which the Spirit makes God's activity in an ancient day contemporary with his people in every generation. The worshipper, therefore, is to listen that he may hear God speak as the sacred story is read and as the Word of God is preached; and when he comes to the Eucharist, he will receive the tokens of Christ's death with faith so that he in company with his fellow-believers in heaven and on earth may receive the benefits of Christ's passion to his spiritual nourishment and growth in grace. At various parts of the service he will respond in praise, confession and intercession; most of all in the offering of himself. Yet it is always response to One who has made himself known, whose self-disclosure is recorded in Scripture and proclaimed by the Church. It is because God has spoken to us in his Son that we may respond to him at all; and as we ponder his ways with us, we come to see more and more clearly that if we make any response at all to his self-disclosure in Christ, it is because he has made even our faith possible.

What is in varying ways true of all Christian worship becomes perfectly plain when we consider the true nature of preaching. 'We are ambassadors for Christ, God making his appeal through us. We beseech you on behalf of Christ, be reconciled to God' (II Corinthians 5.20). 'The minister,' says Daniel Jenkins, 'has the dialectical task of so speaking that men hear, not him, but the voice of the living God.'[1] The Word of God by its very nature implies an encounter with the living God; proclaiming God's Word must mean bringing men face to face with Christ. H. H. Farmer describes preaching as

> that divine, saving activity in history, which began two thousand years ago in the advent of Christ and in his personal relationships with men and women, and has continued throughout the ages in the sphere of redeemed personal relationships . . . now focusing on me. . . . This focusing on me is not apart from what has gone before, nor can it be, for it is part of the continuous purpose throughout the years which began in Christ; hence preaching is telling me something. But it is never merely *telling me* something. It is God actively probing me, challenging my will, calling on me for decision, offering me his succour.[2]

[1] D. T. Jenkins, *Tradition and the Spirit*, p. 186.
[2] H. H. Farmer, *The Servant of the Word*, p. 27.

Preaching, then, is not merely *a* way of declaring religious truth; it is the inevitable way to proclaim the Christian Gospel. The Word does not come to us as mere instruction; and while teaching is always a part of preaching, there is a significant difference between a sermon and a lecture. The Word cannot be given to men with indifference to their response; since God is making the appeal, it is vital that his Word be heard and accepted; yet an enforced response would be no response. It is God's Word, the whole fact of his redeeming grace, brought to bear on me; and it is a matter of life and death.[1]

How any man can be the herald of God is, and must remain, a mystery. We cannot guarantee that every time a man preaches the Gospel the Word of God will be proclaimed; and it is of prime importance that we should realize that no external condition can guarantee that it shall happen. Every church has its very proper ways of seeking to ensure that its preachers shall be faithful stewards of the mysteries. Those who are to be ordained are required to undergo proper theological instruction; the preacher vows that he will be faithful to Holy Scripture; and often he has to subscribe to some subordinate standard of faith as well. Yet, proper and even necessary as all these arrangements are, the Holy Spirit is not bound by any of them.

No external guarantee can be given that when a man preaches he will declare the Word of God; but this does

[1] Gustaf Wingren's *The Living Word* is a recent 'theological study of preaching and the Church' from a Lutheran point of view.

not make any excuse for the neglect of such disciplines as are sometimes held to provide such a guarantee. If they are not decisive for the great act of declaration, they are nevertheless of immense importance in the preparation for it. The preacher cannot proclaim the Word of God unless he has studied the Scriptures, unless his mind has grasped the meaning of the passage to be expounded, and, more important still, seen that passage in the context of the whole story of God's redeeming grace. Nor can he ignore theology, the Church's reflection under the guidance of the Holy Spirit upon the Word given to it by God. He preaches as belonging to the community which has lived upon and been governed by this Word, and he can no more cut himself off from that tradition than he can be liberated from Scripture. Nor is the tradition of the Church contrary to that freedom of the Spirit which gives immediacy to the proclamation and to the hearing of God's Word; for what the preacher declares is not an academic treatise on a particular passage nor a correct exposition of some doctrinal point. It is a word gained from these sources, but spoken to a particular person at a particular place. The preached Word, like a letter, needs a name and address upon it; it is never merely spiritual, intellectual, ethical; it is never vague; it is always present and personal.

If it be objected to this way of understanding preaching that it answers the question how a man can be a herald of God by presupposing a miracle, for that seems to be the logic of arguing that we can never so arrange circumstances that the event is 'bound' to happen, the charge must be admitted; but with this defence, that such an answer accords with the fact that we live and walk by faith and not by sight, that is, without the guarantees which ensure the desired result. God's Word is the gift of his grace to his people and, like all other gifts of grace, it can neither be earned (by providing the right conditions) or demanded (by fulfilling one's duty and so deserving either to hear or to speak it). 'Authoritative preaching,' says Dr Brunner, 'is the free gift of God. We can never "possess" the Word of God; we can only pray that it be granted to us when we have to preach.'[1]

3   The Life of the Church

It is, of course, a quite unreal and unnatural over-simplification of the issue to suggest that the Church is no more than a body of believers which offers worship and listens to sermons! It is, rather, a body with a life to be lived in the service of him whose body it is. Its destiny is to continue within the tensions and ambiguities of history the ministry of its risen and triumphant Lord. It is to do its work as a fellowship of the Holy Spirit in a world which at best only partly wants what it has to give and at worst hates the Gospel of love. If we may say that in each act of worship the Church lives again through the events out of which it springs, and meets again him in whose name it lives and works, we may also say that in the rough and tumble of its actual work among men and women and within human insti-

[1] E. Brunner, *Revelation and Reason*, p. 145.

tutions, it meets the same temptations and obstacles as once beset its Lord, must make for itself the sort of decisions he then had to make, and discover for itself by his Spirit the sort of obedience through which God's grace becomes operative in the world. Here, too, the Church relives the events out of which it was born; the Bible becomes a living book not only because the Holy Spirit reveals its truth in times of worship and Bible study, but also because in the cut-and-thrust of active service he continues his illuminating work. The Bible is never seen to be more relevant, nor its authority more powerful, than when its message breaks in upon my circumstances and my tasks to shed light and bring living power. The testimony of the German Christians who were imprisoned for conscience' sake under the Hitler régime is but one illustration of what Christian people of all types and traditions have known, when their worship has found expression in life and their life has been hallowed by worship. The Word of God has become active for them; through it God has indeed spoken, and the Bible has been the conveyance of his authority.

It is for such reasons as these that we may say that the Christian believer is enabled to understand and receive the Word of God within the Church. The Church in worship and preaching, and in common life, bears witness to the objective facts of God's self-disclosure in history as recorded in Scripture, and the Holy Spirit enables the believer to perceive and accept the divine message which they declare. As Dr Dodd says:

We receive the Bible from the Church: there is no other source from which we can receive precisely *these* writings in *this* setting, which make up the canon of Scripture. It is also the book which contains the history out of which the Church has emerged. The Scriptures are concerned with the continuing life of an historical community—the people of God. This community remains self-identical through many changing historical forms. . . . Every part of that long history—down to the present day—is relevant to the acceptance and understanding of the Bible as the Word of God. Bible and Church are correlatives. The attempt (since the Reformation) to set the authority of the Bible over against that of the Church, and the authority of the Church over against the authority of the Bible, results only in obscuring the nature of this authority, which resides in both together.[1]

4 The Value of Scripture

From this consideration of the relation between Scripture and the Church we may approach the answer to the question: What exactly is the value and meaning of the written Scripture?

'History might be called the sacrament of the religion of Israel; through the history of Israel, she saw the face of God and endured as seeing him who is invisible. But the details of that history . . . the words and deeds, the thoughts and emotions, and above all the persistent purposes of the Israelites—these were the bread and wine of the sacrament, which the touch of God transformed

[1] C. H. Dodd in an essay on 'The Relevance of the Bible', contributed to *Biblical Authority for Today*, ed. A. Richardson and W. Schweitzer, p. 157.

into both the symbol and the instrument of his grace for all time.'[1] These notable words of a great Old Testament scholar and theologian could easily, and without any unfaithfulness to their meaning, be made immediately relevant to the further history of God's activity in history through the Incarnation of his Son and the act of redemption which issued in the formation of the New Israel. The Christian, like the Israelite, looks back to a history in which the face of God is disclosed; and for him the very details of that history are sacramental, being made 'the symbol and the instrument of God's grace for all time'.

Since Christianity is an historical religion and has its roots in certain datable happenings which are believed to have a particular meaning, historical records are of quite primary importance for its very life. That certain events did in fact take place and that they happened in a particular way and in a certain context is bound to be a matter of standing and falling with a religion which centres so much upon the history of Israel, the Incarnation of the Son of God and the creation of the new People of God. Were it possible to prove that Jesus Christ never existed, Christianity would certainly die. Some pious beliefs and moral ideals might remain, for their validity does not necessarily depend on the factual existence of the teacher who is alleged to have put them forth; some mystery-religion might survive which could be sources of some communal and individual religious experience, provided no one knew whether its stories were true and its rites based on reality; but no im-

[1] H. Wheeler Robinson, *The History of Israel*, p. 12.

aginery figure could possibly create an entirely new relationship between God and man and give to the course of history a new and creative turn.

To say that it is of vital importance to Christianity that it should have reliable documents concerning the events from which it takes its origin is not the same, however, as requiring that the documents should be absolutely and factually accurate in every detail. It is not fatal to the historic nature of our religion that we can trace the development of the historical documents of the Old Testament and observe the ways in which various episodes are treated by successive editors—that the comparative statistics of Samuel, Kings and Chronicles indicate rough and ready calculations, so that one account of this or that event does not strictly tally with another. Nor does it destroy the historical value of the Gospels that, as is now evident, the ecclesiastical necessities of the early Church played their part in the shaping of their witness to the life and teaching, death and resurrection of Jesus Christ. Scholars are not at all agreed whether we are in fact provided with the material for reconstructing a 'life' of Jesus. It may be that the pessimism of some is but a passing fashion of contemporary scholarship, and that those who at present contend that, in the face of no matter what difficulty, it is our duty to construct for ourselves as clear a picture of Jesus Christ as possible, will in the end be justified. Nevertheless the broad shape of the events in which the divine revelation took place is not in question; and we have sufficient evidence both of what took place and of what it was taken to mean for us to be confronted by God's revelation of himself in Jesus Christ.[1]

To argue in this way is not to imply that the historical evidence is the sole importance of the written Scriptures. But it is difficult to determine where the historical, the theological and the religious values begin and end, or whether they can ever be really distinguished. If we are right in believing that history is not made of events alone, and that 'to speak of history and revelation through history, two realities must be brought together; raw facts and their interpretation'. The interpretation 'is more important even than the facts, for it is one's idea of an event which assures for it its quality as an historical fact, that is as a decisive fact in the course of events'.[2] If this is so, we shall find it difficult to be certain at what point we have ceased to deal with what may properly be called historical. We shall be dealing with interpretation; and it is the business of the Bible to interpret, as J. K. Mozley argued:

When the Bible is defined as the 'record' of revelation it is important that the word record should not be misunderstood. The Bible is not a record, as the term is used when we speak of a gramophone record. Such a record is good, when it is good, simply as the re-embodiment of the original. All we ask for is that the original should be reproduced with as much accuracy as possible. The gramophone is not there to be an interpreter. But the Bible is constantly exercis-

[1] For a discussion of the theological issues at stake in this problem, compare D. M. Baillie, *God Was in Christ*, p. 30 ff., and also the Appendix to the second edition.
[2] Edmond Jacob, *Theology of the Old Testament*, p. 184.

ing the function of an interpreter: its purpose is to enable and indeed to challenge, men to look on life in a particular way, and that is the way of the Bible's own interpretation. This office of an interpreter runs through the Bible.[1]

On this reckoning, it might well be argued that, at least in a certain sense, witness to the *meaning* of the event is as historical as the record of the 'raw fact', and to declare that Christ crucified is the power of God unto salvation is not less historical than to record that he was crucified between two malefactors. It is clear that all the time the historical is recorded so that its meaning may be conveyed, understood, and accepted (John 20.31). Witness without 'raw fact' might be no more than wishful thinking: and 'raw fact' without interpretation would be meaningless, since without *some* interpretation no 'raw fact' can be understood at all. The supreme value, therefore, of the written Scripture is that it records the mighty acts of God for the redemption of mankind. It tells what happened and what it means; and so it provides for ever the basis upon which the Holy Spirit enables the redeemed community to encounter the living God as made known in Jesus Christ. With the Spirit's light upon them the Scriptures are the means whereby God speaks to men in every generation; and it is in this sense that they are properly called the Word of God.

To conclude: it has been argued in this book that all authority belongs to Christ, that the Bible derives its

[1] J. K. Mozley's essay 'The Bible' in *The Christian Faith*, ed. W. R. Matthews, pp. 51-2.

authority from him, and that the authority of the Bible must be exercised in the same way as Christ exercises his. This has led to an emphasis on the place of an individual believer's perception of truth as an essential element in the whole process of revelation, although this by no means makes light of the part which the Church is called to play in interpreting the Scriptures.

The whole notion of an authoritative canon of Scripture is bound up with the idea of the Church, so that it is not possible to set the authority of Scripture and of the Church over against each other; and if we are to think that both Scripture and Church are means whereby Christ exercises his authority, the whole notion of any essential antagonism between them is not only impossible but ridiculous.

We are thus aware of three centres through which Christ exercises his authority : (1) the Scriptures, (2) the Church and (3) what is sometimes called individual conscience. All three of them are really 'secondary' authorities, for they are only valid and useful, only really authoritative, in so far, and only in so far, as they reflect and make effective the one supreme authority. The deepest religious conviction and assurance are known by those who are aware of no tension between these 'secondary' authorities. When a man's personal convictions are in harmony with the witness of the Scriptures and the *consensus fidelium*,[1] he knows real certainty. This is to know with all the saints what is the breadth and length and depth and heighth, and 'to know the love of Christ which surpasses knowledge'

[1] The agreement of the faithful.

(Ephesians 3.19). The historic and the social nature of Christianity alike require that personal conviction should be at one with the faith once for all delivered to the saints, and with the common experience of all others who have found salvation in Christ. It is when the Bible, the Church, and the believer conspire to say one thing that the authority of Christ is most surely acknowledged.

And Christ's authority is absolutely personal—never abstract, never simply rational, emotional, or ethical. In the Gospel the God-man confronts us with all his immense authority. There is no other ultimate authority. This means that there can be no final external standards of authority, and therefore no final external security. It is the besetting temptation of the Christian believer to find some secondary authority which will appear to afford sufficient security to screen him from the ordeal of personal encounter with Christ himself: the Bible, the Church, even his personal convictions. But *there is no such external authority*, nor can there be, valuable as such 'secondary' authorities are when they minister Christ's authority. The true believer is not one who discourses about what the Bible says, what the Church teaches, or, still worse, 'what I think'. The believer is one who, knowing all that the facts can teach him, not neglecting what his fellows have learned, nor without his own personal convictions as well, lives in constant response to the ever-present Christ. He seeks to understand and obey, to trust and to serve him to whom all authority in heaven and earth has been given.

FOR FURTHER READING

The books listed are the modern ones referred to in the text.

Adam, Karl, *The Spirit of Catholicism*, Sheed and Ward

Baillie, D. M., *God Was in Christ*, Faber and Faber
Baillie, John, *The Idea of Revelation in Recent Thought*, Oxford
Betterson, H., *Documents of the Christian Church*, Oxford
Berdaeyev, N., *Freedom and the Spirit*, Bles
Brunner, E., *Christianity and Civilization*, Lutterworth
Brunner, E., *Revelation and Reason*, SCM Press
Bultmann, R., *Jesus Christ and Mythology*, SCM Press
Burnaby, J., *Is the Bible Inspired?*, Duckworth

Cadoux, C. J., *Catholicism and Christianity*, Allen and Unwin
Catholic Commentary on Holy Scripture, ed. B. Orchard, Nelson
Caird, G. B. *Principalities and Powers*, Oxford
The Christian Faith, ed. W. R. Matthews, Eyre and Spottiswoode
Cunliffe-Jones, H., *The Authority of the Biblical Revelation*, Clarke

Dakin, A., *Calvinism*, Duckworth
Dodd, C. H., *The Authority of the Bible*, Nisbet (also in Fontana Books)
Dodd, C. H., *The Bible Today*, Cambridge

Farmer, H. H., *The Servant of the Word*, Nisbet
Farrer, A. M., *The Glass of Vision*, Bles
Forsyth, P. T., *The Principle of Authority*, Independent Press

Harnack, A., *What is Christianity?* Clarke
Hebert, A. G., *The Authority of the Old Testament*, Faber and Faber
Hebert, A. G., *Fundamentalism and the Church of God*, SCM Press
Hodgson, L., *For Faith and Freedom*, Nisbet
The Interpretation of the Bible, ed. C. W. Dugmore, SPCK

Jacob, E., *Theology of the Old Testament*, Hodder and Stoughton

Jenkins, Daniel, *Tradition and the Spirit*, Faber and Faber

Miegge, G., *The Virgin Mary*, Lutterworth Press

New Bible Commentary, ed. F. Davidson and A. M. Stibbs, Tyndale Press

Oman, John, *Vision and Authority*, Hodder and Stoughton

Packer, J. I., *Fundamentalism and the Word of God*, Tyndale Press

Reid, J. K. S., *The Authority of Scripture*, Methuen
Revelation and the Bible, ed. C. F. H. Henry, Tyndale Press
Richardson, Alan, *Christian Apologetics*, SCM Press
Richardson, Alan, *Preface to Bible Study*, SCM Press

Robinson, H. Wheeler, *Inspiration and Revelation in the Old Testament*, Oxford

Smart, J. D., *The Interpretation of Scripture*, SCM Press

Tasker, R. V. G., *The Old Testament in the New Testament*, SCM Press

Temple, William, *Nature, Man and God*, Macmillan

Warfield, B. B., *The Inspiration and Authority of the Bible*, Marshall, Morgan and Scott

Wenham, J. W., *Our Lord's View of the Old Testament*, Tyndale Press

Williams, R. R., *Authority in the Apostolic Age*, SCM Press
Wingren, G., *The Living Word*, SCM Press

INDEX OF AUTHORS

BULLETIN 148

MAY 1962

SCM Press Ltd

56 Bloomsbury Street

London, WC1

The Religious Book Club

From the Editor's Desk

An Australian Visitor

Less than half an hour ago, an RBC member walked into the office. He is a civil engineer, a lecturer in one of the Australian universities. He reads the RBC books on his bus rides to and from the university. He doesn't stop reading them when he gets out of the bus, so that his absorption in his book during his walk has become a warning to his friends not to interrupt. The traffic seems understanding also!

We always like it when members call on us.

From Our Mail

The Principal of a theological college in Assam, India, writes: 'Your theological publications are a constant source of good scholarship and stimulating thought, and the RBC books and paperbacks provide a good deal of excellent material at reasonable prices for our rather poor students and people. Keep up the good work!'

The Methodist President of another college, in Tonga in the Pacific, writes: 'Having the indigenous Church in mind, especially in countries which have recently gained their independence, may I suggest an outline of Christian theology, and introductions to the OT and NT? As long as the approach was clear and fresh with leanings towards the newer Churches, I'm sure most of the regular readers would be interested too. Thank you for all your service to us; I assure you that the college enjoys receiving the RBC books!'

A third member, herself British, has recently been worshipping with an American congregation in Germany. Her experience made her value John Lawrence's recent book, *The Hard Facts of Unity*. She wants an RBC book on American methods of Christian education.

Conservative Evangelicals

may feel that our current book, *The Bible Says*, is unjust to them. We shall be glad to have any reactions from RBC members, and hope to print some. We tried to get three Conservative Evangelical scholars to review the book in this Bulletin, but in each case we were unsuccessful. We at the SCM Press and on the RBC Committee want our cordial relations with Conservative Evangelicals, who belong in considerable numbers to the Club, to continue.

The Free Book

offered to all who enrol a member during May or June is *Hear the Word!* by Heinrich Zador. This new novel about Elijah and Elisha was published in March at 21*s*.

The July Book

is *Beyond Religion* by Daniel Jenkins. This book begins by examining the suggestion, quite frequently made nowadays, that mature Christian faith can exist, and ought to exist, independently of the religious activities with which it has always been closely associated. Four theologians in particular are studied and criticized: Germany's Dietrich Bonhoeffer with his plea for a 'religion-less Christianity'; Switzerland's Karl Barth with his massive attack on religion in the name of faith; America's Paul Tillich with his 'God beyond God'; and Britain's Alec Vidler with his 'holy worldliness'. Mr Jenkins brings the theologians' ideas down to earth. What does all this mean to the layman – to the man of faith in a secular society? What does it mean to the minister of a flourishing suburban church?

This is one of the most thought-provoking books we have had in the RBC for some time. In a way, its theme is the same as *Irreligious Reflections on the Christian Church* by Werner Pelz (January 1959), but that was a book by an Anglican parish priest;

this is a book by a Congregationalist theologian. The Manchester *Guardian* reviewer said of Mr Jenkins (in connection with his recent book *Equality and Excellence*) that he writes with 'the objective common sense of a man from Mars'. To start the debate, the reviewer of *Beyond Religion* in the next Bulletin will be a philosopher, Professor Ronald Hepburn, who has gone 'beyond religion' to agnosticism – which is a position very different from that of Daniel Jenkins!

The September Book

will be *The Christ of Faith and the Jesus of History* by Dr Gabriel Hebert, whose *When Israel Came Out of Egypt* was such a success as the RBC book last July.

David L. Edwards

The Bishop of Manchester writes about 'The Bible Says'

This is a book which within a small compass covers a wide field, yet it does so without superficiality. The attitudes of churches, sects and individual theologians towards the Bible are clearly and sympathetically expounded and reviewed.

Principal Huxtable's answer to the questions raised during the course of his exposition is not an 'either or' but a 'both and'. Christ in his own person is the final authority but that authority is not exercised by the Bible, by the Church, or by the individual conscience enlightened by the Holy Spirit; it is exercised by all three together. The security sought in a purely external authority is illusory. He well says: 'The believer is one who, knowing all the facts can teach him, not neglecting what his fellows have learned, nor without his own personal convictions as well, lives in constant response to the ever-present Christ'.

This is a big little book and one which I hope will be widely read as a preparation for Bible study. In the churches today few things are more to be desired than a return to the study of the Bible. The enormous sales of the New English Bible encourage one to hope that there is a movement in that direction, but this in itself is not enough unless its rightful authority is understood. That is just what Principal Huxtable sets himself to explain concisely, reasonably, and persuasively.

John Huxtable

Trained at the Western College, Bristol, and Mansfield College, Oxford, John Huxtable became a Congregational minister in 1937. He served churches at Newton Abbot in Devon and at Palmers Green in North London, and in 1953 was appointed Principal of New College, London. In this Congregational theological college, which is associated with the Divinity Faculty of the University of London, he teaches Christian doctrine and ethics. He has had many engagements outside his College as preacher, lecturer or administrator, and he is the Chairman of the Congregational Union of England and Wales for 1962–63. Perhaps with memories of his first charge between the rival beauties of Dartmoor and the Devon coast, he gives as his principal hobby 'escaping from London'. This he does with his family when possible.

This is his fifth book, although his first with the SCM Press. The previous titles were *The Faith That is in Us*, *The Promise of the Father*, *The Christian Doctrine of God* and *Like a Strange People*. He is also joint editor of *A Book of Public Worship*, and has edited John Owen's *True Nature of a Gospel Church*, a classic of 17th-century theology.

The Ministry of the Laity

Some words spoken by Dr Klaus von Bismarck at the New Delhi Assembly of the World Council of Churches made a great impression, and are reproduced here from the WCC bulletin *Laity*.

We may define the nature and task of clergy and laity quite differently, some making a clear distinction between the two; others saying that the frontier between them is, and must remain, very fluid. But one thing is our firm conviction: we not only belong together, we complement each other. Together we are God's people, all of us who bear the mark of baptism. Of course we have varied functions and ministries, but all these different ministries find their origin and purpose in Christ's ministry to the world.

We laymen need you our pastors, priests, theologians and church leaders. We could not live and work as Christians in our secular occupations without the Word of God being continuously addressed to us in worship and Christian teaching, without the support of the sacraments, without this liberating opportunity of the confession of sins and the promise of the remission of sin addressed to us by our Lord through your ministry.

But do not forget that from the pulpit you can never fully appreciate, understand and speak to our situation. Even less can you from the pulpit really penetrate the world with Christ's word and act of redemption. This penetration of the world belongs far more to *our* ministry. It is to a great extent through *our* ministry that Christ manifests the cosmic dimension of his victory on the cross. And therefore you need us. You need to listen to us. And take care: you need not only to listen to your lay helpers who sometimes have become 'domesticated and "pastorized" laymen': copies of yourself. You need to listen to Christians who gain their livelihood in a secular vocation and are therefore fully immersed in the structures and powers of secular society. Our Christian ministry in these our secular jobs is a vital complement to your ministries.

This then is our first plea to you: become our partners and let us be your partners. Do not continue to play only solo instruments but let us join into Christ's great orchestra so that *together* we can play the symphony of redemption.

The equipment of the laity

Our second concern is the equipment of the laity for their particular ministry. Much money in our church budgets is being spent for the training of the clergy and their professional and non-professional lay helpers. This is indeed very important. But do you spend at least as much money for the equipment of those Christians who try to do God's work in a secular job and who after all form about 99 per cent of the church membership?

In this equipment Bible study is of great importance. But Bible study means for us not listening to a double sermon or just learning a bit of the academic exegesis which you have learnt in your theological colleges. Bible study for us means listening to God's Word spoken into our concrete life and work situation. For this study you must become our teachers and partners. Yet how few pastors have learnt to lead this kind of Bible study and to participate in it!

But Bible study is not enough. To the equipment of the laity belongs also the opportunity for laymen to examine their life situation in the light of Christ's cosmic redemption. In this way we can help one another to be obedient to our Lord in our daily decisions.

Do not misunderstand us. We are not expecting from you the formulation of general Christian principles which often are rather a hindrance than a help. What we need, and what we plead for, are opportunities within the life and structure of our churches where we can critically reconsider the accepted criteria, norms and customs in Church and world; opportunities where, in the light of Christ's ministry, we can examine the decisions and attitudes in our secular work. We need occasions when our ethical imagination can be trained and exercised so that in the thick of our daily life we may make fewer wrong and disobedient choices.

But even with our best equipment our hands will get dirty. The most important element of this equipment of the laity is therefore a constant reminder that we have a gracious Father to whom we can confess our sins and who gives us the courage and joy to proceed from error to error, from dilemma to dilemma, in his way.

With such words – and, indeed, with some of Principal Huxtable's remarks in *The Bible Says* – may be linked the opening words of *Church Order in the New Testament* by Professor Eduard Schweizer (1961, 16s):

There is no such thing as *the* New Testament Church order. Even in NT times the relationships were very varied, and it may be vital for the ecumenical dialogue that we should admit this. Does this mean that every Church order, from the Quakers' to the Roman Catholics', is equally justified in taking its stand on the NT?

The answer depends on the way in which we regard the NT as an authority. Its content would be misunderstood if we regarded its Church order as a *law* that we had to imitate. For even in the NT the ordering of the church in Jerusalem is not a law for the church in Corinth; and Luke, who was the first to reflect on the question of the Church's historical development, seems consciously to distinguish between the time when the Church began and the later time, and to see different laws operating in two periods. Still less can we take our stand on OT laws.

This does not mean, however, that Church order is a matter of indifference, or is to be dictated simply by the existing practical, political, or economic conditions. The NT's pronouncements on Church order are to be read as a *gospel*—that is, Church order is to be regarded as a part of the proclamation in which the Church's witness is expressed, as it is in its preaching. There may be times when this kind of proclamation is better heard and regarded by the world than are any words; and for that reason this part of the Church's witness must be given clearly and plainly. Certainly the church that lacks order does not cease to be a church, but its service is impaired.

Christian Worship in India

A group of Indian theologians and a few missionaries has produced a rather exciting report called *Christian Worship in India*. I came across it at the headquarters of the World Council of Churches. (Perhaps the Faith and Order Secretary at 17 Route de Malagnou, Geneva, would supply copies if asked nicely and with some small financial contribution!)

I picked out the question: can the Church's worship be made really Indian? These theologians find the idea of using Indian music easiest, and they say that there is already a rich collection of Christian lyrics in the regional languages. They want Western hymns still to be available to Indian worshippers, 'but the richness of meaning and depth of theological insights need not be associated with particular tunes.' They want the indigenous customs of story singing to be used more in Christian teaching.

Washing and the removal of the shoes before prayers, sitting on the floor or prostration during worship, the use of flowers, lights and incense, Indian architecture, perhaps even some use of non-Christian scriptures – these are also commended. It is pointed out that some Hindu words, 'From darkness lead them to light; from death lead them to everlasting life', are already in the Church of South India's service for Baptism, and that India has more than one Christian Ashram (monastic centre).

The group also urges the honouring of Indian heroes of the faith, and Christian use of Indian festivals such as the harvest festivals or Dipavali the beautiful Hindu festival of lights before winter begins. Pooja, with its religious dedication of tools, etc., might become the Indian Rogationtide. It is pointed out that Christmas Day was originally a secular feast in Rome! The report closes with a bibliography showing how much thinking has been going on along these lines. For this we must congratulate Roman Catholics as well as other Indian Christians.

D. L. E.

Printed in England by Staples Printers Limited at their Rochester, Kent, establishment.